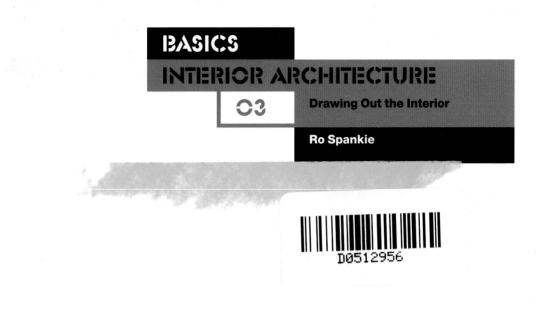

BASICS

INTERIOR ARCHITECTURE

03   Drawing Out the Interior

Ro Spankie

An AVA Book

Published by AVA Publishing SA
Rue des Fontenailles 16
Case Postale
1000 Lausanne 6
Switzerland

Tel: +41 786 005 109
Email: enquiries@avabooks.ch

Distributed by Thames & Hudson (ex-North America)
181a High Holborn
London WC1V 7QX
United Kingdom

Tel: +44 20 7845 5000
Fax: +44 20 7845 5055
Email: sales@thameshudson.co.uk
www.thamesandhudson.com

Distributed in the USA and Canada by:
Ingram Publisher Services Inc.
1 Ingram Blvd.
La Vergne, TN 37086
USA

Tel: +1 866 400 5351
Fax: +1 800 838 1149
Email:
customer.service@ingrampublisherservices.com

English Language Support Office
AVA Publishing (UK) Ltd.

Tel: +44 1903 204 455
Email: enquiries@avabooks.ch

ISBN 2-940373-88-4 and 978-2-940373-88-8

10 9 8 7 6 5 4 3 2 1

Design by John F McGill

Production by
AVA Book Production Pte. Ltd., Singapore

Tel: +65 6334 8173
Fax: +65 6259 9830
Email: production@avabooks.com.sg

Drawing Out the Interior

Name:
House

Location:
London, England

Date:
1993

Designer:
Rachel Whiteread

Contents

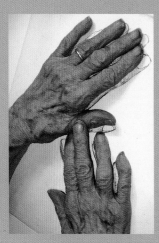

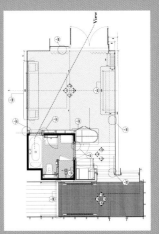

Contents

Introduction

The aim of this book is to provide an introduction to representing interior space through drawing and model. Interior architecture is a discipline concerned with form, structure and material, and how we occupy and understand the space around us. This sets a challenge in terms of representation, as one is not merely drawing form but also the space that it contains. The form appears as lines on the paper but raises the question, how is space given presence on the page?

In setting out to answer this question this book roughly follows the design process. Explaining through example, it introduces the reader to a range of techniques and types of drawing and an understanding of when to use them. Starting with why designers draw in the first place, this book goes on to explore what one might draw and when.

The book begins with initial ideas – literally thinking through the act of drawing – to the design development; testing ideas through scale and measure. Later sections look at drawing space in the third dimension with perspective and model that are more realistic to the eye yet not necessarily to scale. The final sections look at how one might begin to represent more ephemeral qualities such as light and colour. These drawings tend to be more qualitative than quantitative and make reference to other disciplines such as fine art or film. Of course, individual designers all work in their own way – some starting with a model, others with a line – so there is no hard and fast rule.

Most drawings can be drawn in many ways; a plan for instance can be hand drawn in pencil, ruled in ink or constructed as part of a three-dimensional model in a software package. This book is not a manual of graphic techniques but is a reference and inspiration to the types of drawing and ways of making images available. It is not just about representation – the method we choose to draw with influences the way we think and therefore what we design.

Name:
Scena per angola (proposed two-point perspective system for backdrops in stage design)

Location:
N/A

Date:
1711

Designer:
Ferdinando Galli-Bibiena

Drawing Out the Interior

How to get the most out of this book

This book introduces different aspects of the representation of interior space through drawing and models, via dedicated chapters for each topic. Each chapter provides clear examples from leading architectural practices, annotated to explain the reasons behind the design choices made.

Section headers
Each chapter is broken down into sub-sections, the title of which can be found at the top left-hand corner of each spread.

Section introduction
Each sub-section is introduced by a short paragraph, outlining the content to be covered.

Page numbers
Page numbers are displayed in the top right-hand corner of each spread.

Detail drawing, as the name suggests, is the drawing of elements of a proposal at a detailed or large scale (1:1, 1:2, 1:5) in order to explore and explain how different materials fit together. Like anatomical drawings, details reveal the secrets of construction, the art of joining and the hidden geometries that are not apparent in the completed proposal. Because of this they are usually drawn with orthographic techniques that cut and reveal, such as plan, section or exploded axonometric.

Detail on scale of body

Name:
Paimio Sanitorium

Location:
Paimio, Finland

Date:
1933

Designer:
Alvar Aalto

'The main purpose of the building is to function as a medical instrument... one of the basic prerequisites for healing is to provide complete peace... The room design is determined by the depleted strength of the patient, reclining in his bed. The colour of the ceiling is chosen for quietness, the light sources are outside the patient's field of vision, the heating is orientated to the patient's feet and the water runs soundlessly from the taps to make sure no patient disturbs his neighbour.'

The above quote from the Finnish architect Alvar Aalto reveals the intent behind the detailing for Paimio Sanatorium. The surface of the washbasin shown is carefully angled to silence running water as it falls into the basin below: Aalto is not just detailing a washbasin but also a general atmosphere of peace for the patient. The smallest detail affects the whole.

Above:
Photograph of washbasin
Aalto wanted to create washbasins that would allow water to run soundlessly, thus maintaining a calm and peaceful atmosphere for patients at the Paimio Sanitorium.

'The details establish the formal rhythm, the building's finely fractionated scale. Details when they are successful are not mere decoration. They do not distract or entertain. They lead to an understanding of the whole of which they are an inherent part.'
Peter Zumthor

Constructing a detail

To draw details requires knowledge of materials, their dimensions and how elements come together, and this can make them intimidating drawings for a student. However, once it is understood that drawing a detail is as much about research and an understanding of the desired end effect as it is about the actual act of drawing, details can become one of the most poetic and enjoyable types of drawing.

Detail drawings can be drawn on a computer, with a ruler, or freehand. Some of the best details are drawn with a blunt pencil on the back of an envelope in response to an issue on site. There are graphic conventions to indicate materials and it is usual to use text as well as graphic. The text both confirms drawn elements (for example, 'countertop 50mm timber') and describes things that are difficult to draw (for example 'with rounded pencil edge'). It must be clear which graphic the text is referring to. The detail should always refer back to the bigger picture and be able to be located on an overall plan or section. There are various conventions for this and people have a style of detailing.

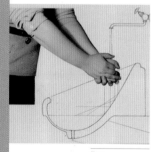

Above:
Section through washbasin
Ink, pencil, and photo collage on board, describing the detail of the washbasins.

Drawing to measure

*Axonometric and Isometric > **Detail** > Survey drawing*

Chapter footers
The current chapter is displayed in the bottom left-hand corner of each spread.

Boxed texts
Additional points of interest to the reader are displayed in grey boxes

The examples shown include a mix of photographs, sketches and drawings, which, when combined with detailed analysis in the text, create a unique and fascinating insight into the world of interior architecture.

Captions
All captions carry a directional and title for easy reference.

Pull quotes
Additional quotes from subject experts and practitioners.

Right:
Exterior of south wall
Note how windows appear as black openings.

Below:
Interior of south wall image
The same wall from the inside – the windows radiate light while the wall appears dark.

Below:
Drawing of interior of south wall
The surfaces of the window openings are painted white and the openings themselves are cut out.

'This was the genius of our ancestors, that by cutting off the light from this empty space they imparted to the world of shadows that formed there a quality of mystery and depth superior to that of any wall painting or ornament.'

Junichiro Tanizaki

Drawing in shadow

Name:
Pilgrimage Chapel of Notre Dame at Ronchamp
Location:
France
Date:
1954
Designer:
Le Corbusier

In 1933 the Japanese novelist Junichiro Tanizaki wrote an essay on aesthetics called *In Praise of Shadows*. Widely read, the essay describes the difference between the shadowy world of traditional Japanese interiors and the dazzling light of the modern age, arguing that darkness is a difficult subject for architecture and design and its benefits are often unfairly stigmatised.

Shadow makes light visible and many architects and designers have used this to great effect in interiors where it is possible to control the amount of light and shadow. A beautiful example might be Le Corbusier's Pilgrimage Chapel at Ronchamp. Light passing through the coloured glass windowpanes pours colour on to the rough concrete wall openings. In drawings of the south wall from the exterior the windows are shown as dark holes in a white surface. In the drawing of the interior elevation of the south wall, the white surface of the openings is literally painted on to a dark outline elevation. The window openings themselves have been cut out of the paper and the location of the small coloured pieces of glass are marked with pencil on transparent tracing paper that is placed behind the window holes. It has been suggested 'as if the drawing could be held up to the light to test the effect of the design.'

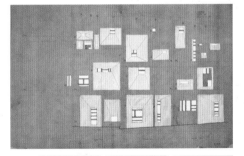

Far left and left:
Light detail
Pink and blue light is emitted into the interior.

Drawing effect

Light > Colour

How to get the most out of this book

Case study information
Each case study is introduced by name, location, date and designer.

Section footers
Past, present and future sub-sections are listed in the bottom right-hand corner of each spread. The current sub-section is highlighted in bold.

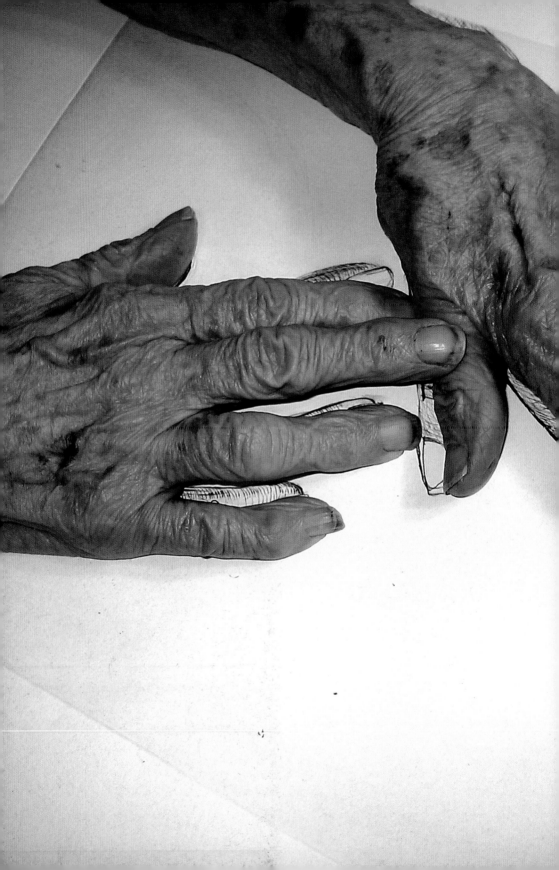

This section will introduce the reader to the core assumptions that underpin interior architecture. It will ask what interior architecture is and look at what a drawing is and why it is that designers draw. Introducing the idea of drawing as a mode of enquiry and means of communication, it will consider the conventions and techniques that are relevant to the task; who is the drawing for and where is it appropriate to experiment?

Name:
Louise Bourgeois' hands placed over one of her etchings in 2003.
Photo: Felix Harlan

Interior architecture, interior design and interior decoration are all terms describing the creation of internal space. Differences between the terms have more to do with the scale of the intervention than with the intent. Interior architecture implies that the intervention will have architectural scale to it, including the manipulation of structural elements such as walls, floors and staircases. Interior design engages at the scale of an individual space so will include the arrangement of built-in elements and more mobile furniture, while interior decoration is concerned with surface effect. The terms apply to proposals within both existing and new buildings. All three are concerned with not just physical intervention but also with how space is understood and occupied, which are described here as form and effect.

For clarity, the person designing the spaces is referred to as the designer although they might be an architect, an interior architect, an interior designer, decorator or even a DIY enthusiast.

Below:
Lina Loos' bedroom, 1903
Loos argued that the creation of a space should be driven primarily by the effect that the designer wishes to exert on the spectator. For his wife's bedroom, Loos covered the floor in blue carpet overlain with white angora fleece, and covered the walls in Batiste rayée to create a 'feminine' effect.

The design process

Form

Form is matter. Or put another way, form is the physical material elements of a scheme. Form includes both structural elements and surface finish. It is both the architectural envelope and the more scenographic elements that define how the space is used. Form encloses space and by doing so gives space its shape. It could be described as the primary material of the interior architect. Although form exists in three dimensions it can be described in two dimensions through various geometrical techniques of orthographic projection, such as plan and section.

Effect

The architect and theorist, Adolf Loos, pointed out that architecture is not just about form. He argued that the creation of space should be driven primarily by the effect that the designer wishes to exert upon the spectator. According to Loos, the architect or designer's 'general task is to provide a warm liveable space. Carpets are warm and liveable. He decides for this reason to spread out one carpet on the floor and to hang up four to form the four walls. But you cannot build a house out of carpets. Both the carpet on the floor and the tapestry on the wall require a structural frame to hold them in the correct place. To invent this frame is the architect's second task.'

'But the artist, *the architect*, first senses the effect that he wishes to exert upon the spectator… These effects are produced both by the material and the form of the space.'

Adolf Loos

What does Loos mean by effect? The effect is the experience, reading or emotional response a space induces in the user. It is created by qualities such as material, light and colour as well as association and memory. It can be an overwhelming or just a gradual sense, but it is the quality that allows us to use subjective terms such as 'cheerful' or 'warm' in describing an interior. In designing effect, form matters, specifically the relationship between forms. In comparison to form, the effect is less quantifiable, so more challenging to represent. But it is precisely with these drawings that the skill of the interior architect lies.

So interior architecture is the art of creating space inside the architectural envelope. The space is constructed by form but is read and understood through effect. Interior architecture and design as a discipline has always been difficult to define because of its double identity both as actual and perceived space, both as formal proposition and as image or effect. More dynamic and fluid than the structure that contains it, an interior, like a stage set, forms the backdrop to everyday life.

What is interior architecture? > Why draw?

What is interior architecture?
Focus study 1

Name:
Puppet theatre in Wapping
Hydraulic Power Station

Location:
London , England

Date:
2004

Designer:
Dan Deng (masters interior
design student at the University
of Brighton, England)

This thesis project for a children's
puppet theatre was inspired by
the discovery that the Wapping
Hydraulic Power Station had once
powered the stage curtains and
machinery of some of London's
West End theatres. Work was
preceded by the construction
of a viewing machine to map the
existing interior. Later these ideas
were developed into and around
a series of 'red curtains' which
bring into question the position
of backstage and front of house,
actor and audience, allowing
the children to participate in the
magic of puppeteering.

Above:
Perspective
Perspective is used to
describe space as it is seen,
the relationship between old
and new, and effects such
as materiality, colour and light.

Left:
Plan
The plan is a horizontal cut
through the building and shows
form and layout.

The design process

'There's the outside of the outside form, the inside of the outside form, and then a space in perpetual tension. Then there's the outside of the inside form and finally, the inside of the inside form... Inside and outside are both coincidental and discontinuous. Fit and misfit.'

Eric Owen Moss

Below:
Section
The section is a vertical cut showing form and volume. By using collaged elements, the section also begins to show how the space is occupied.

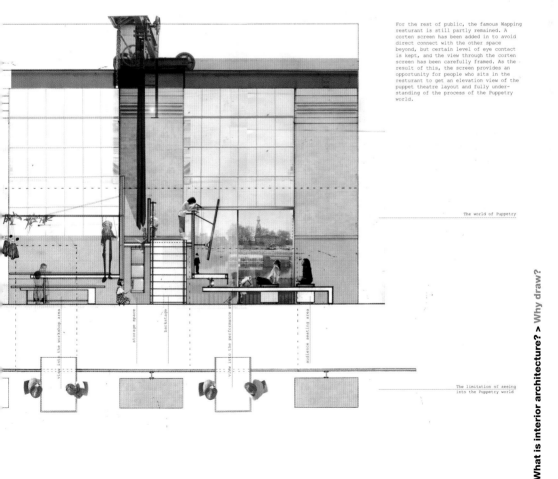

For the rest of public, the famous Wapping resturant is still partly remained. A corten screen has been added in to avoid direct connect with the other space beyond, but certain level of eye contact is kept, and the view through the corten screen has been carefully framed. As the result of this, the screen provides an opportunity for people who sits in the resturant to get an elevation view of the puppet theatre layout and fully understanding of the process of the Puppetry world.

The world of Puppetry

The limitation of seeing into the Puppetry world

view into the workshop area

storage space

backstage

view into the performance stage

audience seating area

What is interior architecture? > Why draw?

The first question an aspiring interior architect might ask is 'why draw?' There is no rule saying we need to draw. Vernacular architecture and interiors have been built for centuries without need for the lengthy and skilled process of drawing. Many interiors simply evolve through generations of use. This section explores briefly why drawing has emerged historically and will give an understanding as to why designers draw.

Drawing through history

Up until the fifteenth century the three visual arts – architecture, painting and sculpture – were not seen as intellectual activities but as mechanical skills confined to artisan guilds. Full-size templates were used to describe important features such as a column capital, but drawings in the sense we understand them were not an important part of the building process. It was possible to build without drawings or models because the designer and the maker were often one and the same person and the desire for innovation was localised.

However, during the Renaissance a shift in this paradigm appeared as designing and making became separate professions. Around this time the image of the architect became identified by the roll of paper and drafting tools in their hand. The command of drawing distinguished the designer from the other occupations involved in the building process.

There are two reasons behind this shift. Firstly, the rediscovery of perspective resulted in a change in the status of the drawing. For the first time there was an understanding that the drawing was an accurate representation of the world around it and therefore could be a useful tool. Secondly the term 'designer' came into being. Derived from the Italian word *disegno* meaning 'drawing', the term suggests both the drawing of a line on paper and the drawing forth of an idea from the mind. Embodied in this concept was the assumption that the act of designing was a separate activity to the act of making and that intellectual labour was superior to manual labour.

Opposite page:
Treatise on projective geometry
In 1648 Abraham Bosse published a series of illustrations in the book, *Maniere Universelle de Monsieur Desargues*. This was the first treatise on projective geometry.

The design process

'... the architect never works directly on the object of their thought, always working at it through some intervening medium, almost always the drawing.'

Robin Evans

'I want to see things,
that's why I draw.
Things show to me
only when I draw them.'

Carlo Scarpa

To design

So what does a designer do? What is design? To map out in the mind, to plan and propose, to invent, to draw, to project, to describe or to scheme? Probably all of these. The act of drawing, regardless if it is with pencil, keyboard or other medium, is a combination of the eye, the mind, the imagination and the hand. It is an intellectual activity that links sensing, feeling, thinking and doing. When ideas are at the embryonic stage there can be an almost subconscious dialogue between impulse, ideas and marks, the brain receiving feedback from marks appearing on the page. Drawing becomes a mode of thinking. In the twenty-first century the concept of *disegno* has become so integral to the definition of designer that the ability to think through drawing has become the true mark of the professional designer.

To innovate

Many artefacts are created without drawings or other external representations. Changes are introduced by trial and error over generations in response to change in use. Trial and error is fine if there is no desire to innovate; to produce something new.

When a client employs an interior architect there is an understanding not only of the cultural value of design but also a desire for innovation and the one-off. Interiors are rarely designed independently of context or as a mass product because they are responding to and are influenced by the building in which they sit. They are bespoke. Buildings are large and expensive and any design proposition involves the employment and labour of many different professions and trades. It is therefore highly valuable to have drawings or models that allow clients to discuss, evaluate, and approve the plans before investing their money, and that allow designers to explain their proposals to the builders so they can specify the parts and coordinate the different building processes.

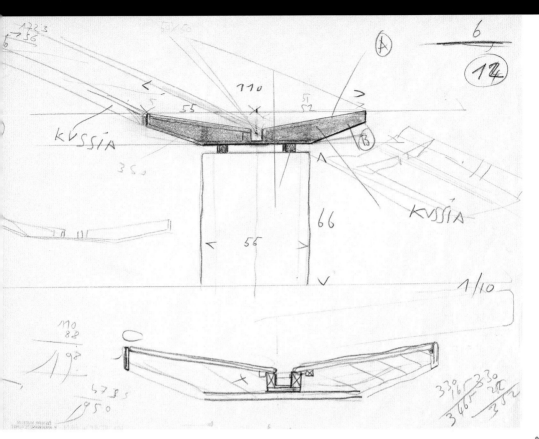

Why draw? Focus study 1

Name:
Palazzo Querini Stampalia

Location:
Venice, Italy

Date:
1963

Designer:
Carlo Scarpa

When Carlo Scarpa was asked to renovate the Palazzo Querini Stampalia in his hometown of Venice he worked closely with local craftsmen. The design was a series of discrete interventions within the old structure – clearly distinguishable as modern yet designed with respect for the existing architecture. Each intervention – even the doors – was designed specifically for its location. Cabinetmaker Saverio Anfodillo remembers Scarpa often worked freehand, 'almost as if he was painting', using the drawings to discuss and solve problems, and to explain what he wanted, sometimes making four or five drafts of the same piece.

Above:
Sketch of benches
Sketch of the visitor benches at Palazzo Querini Stampalia, with material specifications and measurements. Scarpa created this drawing using sketching paper, pencil and orange and yellow crayons.

The *Oxford English Dictionary* defines the verb 'to draw' thus:

Produce a picture or diagram by making lines and marks on paper with a pencil, pen, etc.

Left:
***A woman sewing
in an interior,***
Vilhelm Hammershøi, 1901
When the Danish artist Vilhelm Hammershøi put brush to canvas he set out to capture something of what he saw in the room. The painting refers to his apartment in Copenhagen but is neither a precise description of it nor a proposal of how it should look. The painting itself is the product.

Representation

What is a drawing? The answer is not as simple as it might seem. A drawing is traditionally understood as a representation of something real or imagined. When the artist puts brush to canvas, the painting is the product they set out to create. In the same way, if a sculptor fashions a piece of stone it becomes the sculpture.

A designer works differently to an artist. The drawing is a description of a proposition rather than an observation. Designers make drawings or models to communicate their ideas to the wider world, the drawing acting like a set of instructions so the design can be realised. As the French designer Philippe Starck said, 'I am my brain's publisher'.

The design process

'God created paper for the purpose of drawing architecture on it. Everything else is at least for me an abuse of paper.'

Alvar Aalto

The process by which an idea in one's head, in one's 'mind's eye', is translated into inhabitable space is often long and literally drawn out. The realisation of any three-dimensional design proposition is extremely complex, as is its description so that it can be built. In this context drawings are used both as a construction tool and a language to communicate, paradoxically both an invention and a recording. In the description of built form it is quite usual to use many types of drawing, models, text, or even full scale mock-ups.

Below:
Projection and its analogues,
Robin Evans, 1995
This diagram attempts to explain the relationship between the imagination, orthographic drawings (such as plan and section), perspective and the designed object. Evans describes the connecting lines as 'projections' that attempt to bridge the gaps, his point being there will always be a gap between the imagination, the image and the object.

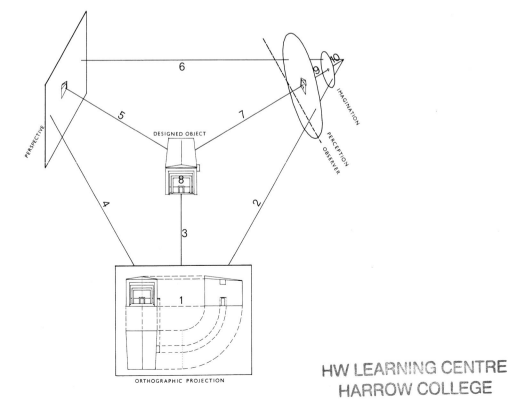

DESIGNED OBJECT

PERSPECTIVE

IMAGINATION

PERCEPTION

OBSERVER

ORTHOGRAPHIC PROJECTION

HW LEARNING CENTRE
HARROW COLLEGE

Why draw? > **What is a drawing?** > Drawing conventions

What is drawing?
Focus study 1

Name:
'Drawing as process and
spatial generator'

Location:
Melbourne, Australia

Date:

2007

Designer:
Danielle Midalia (third-year
interior design student,
RMIT Melbourne, Australia)

In her third-year project, 'Drawing
as process and spatial generator',
Danielle Midalia explored the
use of various types of line
drawing in the design process.
To begin with, sketches were
drawn by hand on-site. These
were then abstracted by
separating horizontal and vertical
lines before being plotted on to
a computer. Finally, these plots
were sent to a CNC router to
produce a model. The translation
between each stage of drawing
was thus used as a generative
tool in the design process.

**Above, left and below:
Sketches**
Hand-drawn sketch (above);
abstracted horizontal lines
from the initial sketches (left);
abstracted vertical lines
from the initial sketches
(left, below); plotted horizontal
and vertical lines (below, left);
plot sent to CNC router
(below, right).

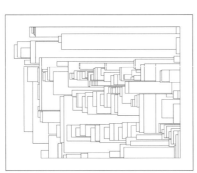

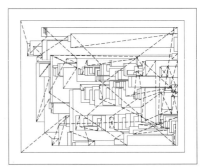

'I like drawing and talking. You have your pen out and say, "well it could be this or it could be that and, by the way, if you know such and such a building" to your client or student and ask, "have you been in the Palm House at Kew?" Then you draw a little bit of a reminder and you progress from that into something else…'

Peter Cook

Tool

The drawing itself can be understood as a tool in the sense that it facilitates the translation of the design idea into built form; from mind to matter. The designer constructs the design on the page, not on the building site, firstly externalising initial thoughts in sketch form, then testing the ideas, evaluating solutions and solving problems before they occur. Drawing out ideas allows the designer to imagine, to fantasise and to speculate on various alternatives, and it is in this context that the drawing is sometimes described as a 'critical tool' or 'site of speculation'. Like any tool it requires knowledge of technique and takes practice. If at first it can seem cumbersome, once mastered many designers find they cannot think without a pen or a mouse in their hand.

Language

Drawing is often described as a graphic language and those who draw as design literate. This is because the other role of drawing is communication. Line and tone have extraordinary conceptual power and can explain a space far quicker than words. The design process involves many conversations: between the design team, then with the client, statutory authorities, contractors, and builders and later perhaps for publication. Each of these parties has different interests and requires a different type of drawing and information.

Thinking drawings are quick and expressive while presentation drawings to the client tend to be three-dimensional and show effect. Working drawings for the contractor are drawn to measure and show how things are constructed and put together. Drawings for publication or student presentations tend to be more conceptual and might represent the ideas behind the proposal.

Below:
Model
Model being produced.

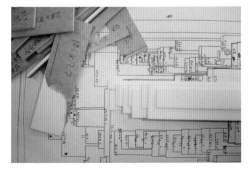

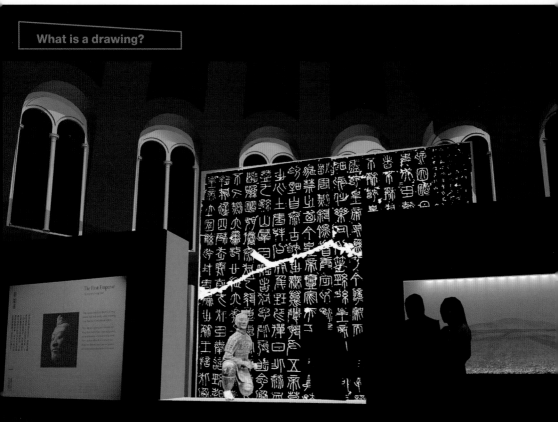

What is a drawing?

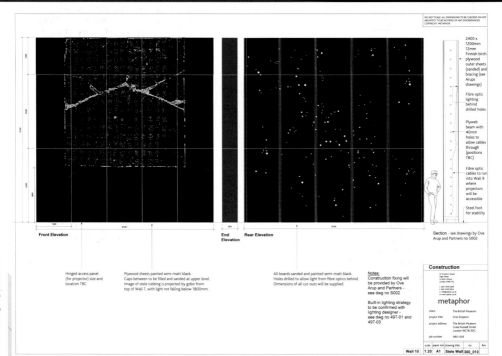

The design process

Front Elevation

End Elevation

Rear Elevation

2400 x 1200mm 12mm Finnish birch plywood outer sheets (sanded) and bracing (see Arups drawings)

Fibre optic lighting behind drilled holes

Plyweb beam with 40mm holes to allow cables through (positions TBC)

Fibre optic cables to run into Wall 9 where projectors will be accessible

Steel foot for stability

Section - see drawings by Ove Arup and Partners no S002

DO NOT SCALE. ALL DIMENSIONS TO BE CHECKED ON SITE
ARCHITECT TO BE NOTIFIED OF ANY DISCREPANCIES
COPYRIGHT: METAPHOR

Hinged access panel (for projector) size and location TBC.

Plywood sheets painted semi-matt black. Gaps between to be filled and sanded at upper level. Image of stele rubbing is projected by gobo from top of Wall 7, with light not falling below 1800mm.

All boards sanded and painted semi-matt black. Holes drilled to allow light from fibre optics behind. Dimensions of all cut outs will be supplied.

Notes:
Construction fixing will be provided by Ove Arup and Partners - see dwg no S002

Built-in lighting strategy to be confirmed with lighting designer - see dwg no 497-01 and 497-03

Construction

47 St John's Wood
High Street
St John's Wood
London NW8 7NJ

t 020 7449 2849
f 020 7449 2824
e info@mphor.co.uk
w www.mphor.co.uk

metaphor

client	The British Museum
project title	First Emperor
project address	The British Museum Great Russell Street London WC1B 3DG
job number	BRI1-003

| | Wall 10 | scale 1:20 | paper size A1 | drawing title Stele Wall | no. 300_010 | Rev |

Opposite page top:
Digital model
Computer model of the Stele
Wall looking at lighting effects.

Opposite page bottom:
Detail drawing
Construction drawing of the
Stele Wall, drawn in Vectorworks.

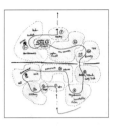

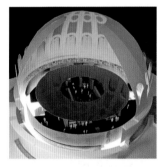

What is drawing?
Focus study 2

Name:
The First Emperor: China's
Terracotta Army exhibition,
The British Museum

Location:
London, England

Date:
2007

Designer:
Metaphor

When the British Museum
approached exhibition designers
Metaphor to design an exhibition
for the Terracotta Army, they
produced a whole series of
drawings. Starting with an initial
concept diagram explaining the
Terracotta Army's role in guarding
the Emperor in the afterlife, this
was developed into an exhibition
layout, including visitor route,
a series of exhibition display
elements such as the Stele
Wall, lighting, projections and
the placing of the artefacts
themselves. All of this had
to be designed in the existing
context of the British Museum's
Round Reading Room.

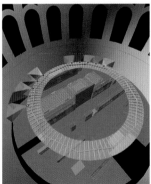

Top left:
Concept diagram
Initial concept, drawn in
Adobe Illustrator.

Top right:
Design drawing
Design drawing showing
initial layout and route. Drawn
with pen and coloured pencil.

Above left:
Model
Model showing crowd
control analysis.

Above right:
Layout
Plan of exhibition layout showing
route, drawn in Vectorworks and
Adobe Illustrator.

Left top:
Presentation model
Cut away model for client
presentation.

Left bottom:
Three-dimensional drawing
Three-dimensional drawing
explaining structure of overhead
ring and projection rig.

Why draw? > **What is a drawing?** > Drawing conventions

Design, like any other discipline, has its own codes and conventions. The process of architectural production, due to the professional need to quantify the parts and to predict the end result, adheres to accepted standard representational conventions. These are sometimes referred to as design 'language'. It is important when one is learning these skills to understand the language before experimenting with it and making it your own. This section looks at generic conventions applicable to the design drawing.

Above:
Stonehouse, Günther
Domenig, 1986–2008
Wireframe computer drawing of Domenig's Stonehouse; 'a place where expression and contents merge' and which 'explores the other aspect of geometry'.

'How and why we make a drawing
or model… are directly related to our
philosophy of architecture. Is design
a process or a product, an image or an
idea, an art or a service?'

Thomas Fisher

Technique

The construction of images has always
been driven by the tools available,
technological advances and shifts in
geometrical understanding. There have
been two major revolutions in the history
of drawing technique. Firstly, in the
Renaissance the rediscovery of linear
perspective; secondly and more recently,
the digital revolution and the simultaneous
rise of virtual reality and computer-based
design and manufacturing. Changes
in technique result not only in changes
in drawing conventions but also in what is
drawn. Thus, as the Renaissance architect
changed from the master craftsman
to designer, the focus of their drawings
shifted from mass and matter to form and
proportion. The arrival of the computer has
resulted in designers becoming interested
in time, emergence, dynamic modelling,
and increasingly sophisticated three-
dimensional form inconceivable 20 years
ago. This is largely due to the ability of new
software to represent these concepts. As
the architectural writer William Mitchell has
observed, architects draw what they can
build, but also build what they can draw.

Style

Drawings, like the propositions they refer
to, have a style. Tom Porter has suggested
that designers develop a drawing style
that is both idiosyncratic and recognisably
their own. However designers also
belong to their time and style is historically
specific. It is therefore possible to recognise
a Beaux Art section, a modernist plan
or the distinctive smooth curvilinear effect
of a software program like Rhino. Having
a recognisable style will bring with it the
connotations and ideology associated
with that style.

Likeness

Design drawings do not have to look like
the intended proposal and can use both
abstract and realistic conventions. Most
orthographic projections such as plan
or section fall into the abstract category
because they are a two-dimensional cut
through the intended form offering a view
impossible to the human eye. Realistic
techniques attempt a three-dimensional
pictorial likeness of the proposal.
These techniques include perspective,
axonometric and model, but also can
include elevation. Paradoxically, the
abstract orthographic techniques, such
as plan and section, can have a more
precise relationship to built form than those
that attempt likeness because they are
true to scale.

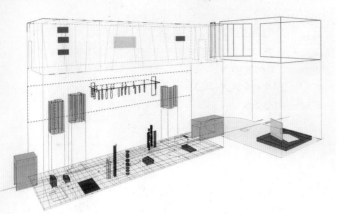

Left:
Strange Kimono exhibition,
Project Orange and
Studio Myerscough, 2000
Design drawing for a proposed
exhibition space at the
Victoria and Albert Museum
in London, England.

Copy and trace

Design drawings are more like musical
scores than paintings because the notion
of 'original' is found in the proposed
scheme rather than the drawing. They
are copies in two senses: firstly because
of the working method known as overlay,
and secondly because design drawings
need be reproduced, printed or photocopied
and distributed to all those involved in the
construction process.

Overlay is a technique, used both on
drawing board and computer, of layering
drawings such as plans or sections on top
of each other and tracing (command 'copy
cut paste') through elements such as walls
or staircases so they line up. The act of
tracing or copying gives the designer time
to think and modify the form – copy as
a creative act.

Intent

However modest the design, a single
drawing will never give a complete
description. There is always a gap between
the drawing and reality, things that are
left out and things that are included.
The convention is to create a package
of drawings where each drawing is given
a purpose. It is important to understand
the purpose and what a drawing needs
to communicate before one begins so the
right information is included. For instance,
a furniture layout does not have to show
structural information.

Text

Some things are hard to describe in drawing
and are better expressed non-graphically.
For example you cannot draw a paint
specification or a concrete mix. Written
text is used on drawings for titles, captions
and dimensions. Some documents such
as specifications and schedules of parts,
which form part of a drawing package, can
be entirely text-based.

The design process

'Architects do not draw space. They concern themselves with the surface of static objects, and assume that the manipulation of space can be achieved through this analogous activity.'

Kevin Rhowbotham

Conventions of interior drawings

The practice of interior architecture operates with representational methods common to architectural practice. However, there are some conventions that are particular to the interior.

Space
Interior drawings are about form and about space. Form is easy to represent in orthographic drawing and model but space remains as white paper in between the black lines. Interior drawings often adopt hybrid techniques such as sectional perspective in order to occupy the space and show effect.

Sequence
Interior architecture cannot be treated as a series of still lifes but rather is experienced as movement through space. Individual moments are not understood in isolation but as part of a sequence of spaces, associations and views.

Effect
Construction of effect is no more accidental than construction of form. Interior drawings should contain the atmosphere we call effect. Techniques include colour, light and shade to give depth, and drawing important objects in space.

Scale
Interiors drawings must work at scale of the space, typically the scale of the building, but also the scale of the object. The furniture and objects that inhabit the space create effect as much as the architecture. For the two to work together both must be drawn.

Viewpoint
Interior architecture is challenging to represent because one is 'thinking inside the box', inside the architectural envelope. In order to show a proposal designers use a variety of conventions: slice open the space, lift the lid, take away a wall, use an x-ray effect or folded wall plan. You can find examples of the use of these conventions throughout the book.

'Drawings of buildings, however slight, give clearer and more permanent ideas than can be obtained from the most detailed, correct and elaborate descriptions.'

Sir John Soane

Drawing conventions:
Focus study 1

Name:
Sir John Soane's Museum

Location:
London, England

Date:
1837

Designer:
Sir John Soane

12/13 Lincoln's Inn Fields was the home of the architect Sir John Soane and his extensive collection of art and antiquities. During his lifetime he constantly rearranged and added to both the interior architecture and the collection, over the years achieving an extraordinary and dense series of spaces. On his death he bequeathed the house as a museum to which 'amateurs and students' should have access. Today behind its classical white Portland stone façade lies one of the most unexpected interiors in London.

Top:
Sketch
A collage of the dome by Negin Moghaddam.

Above:
The dome
Photograph of the dome, looking east with the bust of Sir John Soane in the centre.

Opposite page:
Sectional perspective
Sectional perspective through the dome at 12/13 Lincoln's Inn Fields, painted in watercolour by George Bailey. The technique of colouring the sectional cut pale pink is typical of its style. Note the more conventional plan and section in each corner.

·VIEW· OF· VARIOUS· ·ARCHITECTVRAL· ·SVBIECTS· BELONGING TO ·IOHN·SOANE·ESQ.R R·A· AS ARRANGED IN ·MAY· ·MDCCCX·

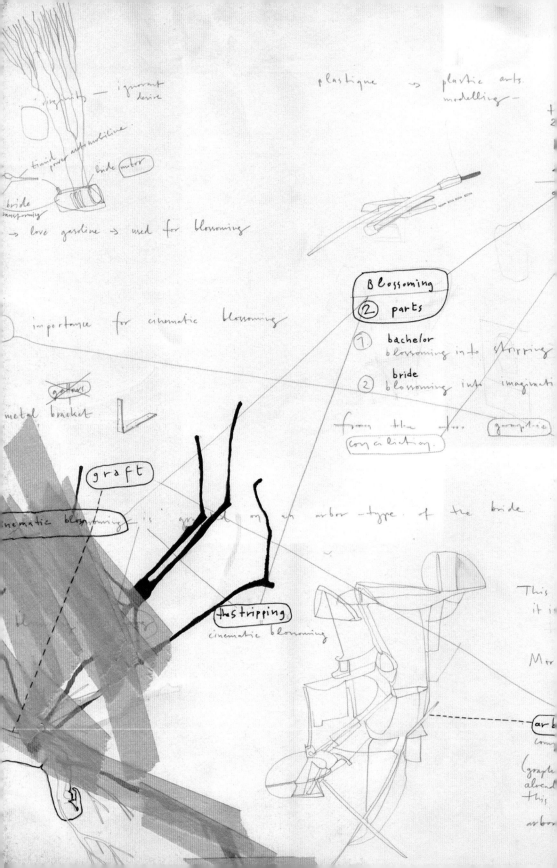

plastique ⇒ plastic arts.
modelling —

illegibility — ignorant desire

timid power automobiline.
bride motor

bride nonconformity

⇒ love gasoline ⇒ used for blossoming

importance for cinematic blossoming

metal bracket

graft

cinematic blossoming is grafted on an arbor-type of the bride.

the stripping
cinematic blossoming

Blossoming
2 parts

1 bachelor
blossoming into stripping

2 bride
blossoming into imaginative

from the above conciliation.

geometric

This
it is

Mor

arb

(graph
above
this
arbor

Ideas are conceived in the mind but the designer
needs to visualise them. 'Thinking drawings'
and 'visual thinking' are terms borrowed from the
field of psychology. They refer to a form of thinking
that uses vision, imagination and drawing and is
usually concerned with the early stages of design.
Ideas can start as words, feelings and images in
the mind: open-ended, loose and fragmented. The
first marks can look nothing like the final product.
Thinking drawings are a method of arranging
disparate ideas on a page so that they can then be
worked out, thought about, drawn, tested, rethought,
redrawn, retested, until they slowly take form.

Form, however – in the sense of proposition – is not
important at this stage. Techniques discussed in
this chapter are more concerned with how to respond
to programme, how space is used, thinking about
time, movement and what might have inspired the
idea in the first place.

Thinking drawings can be quick, sketchy,
diagrammatic and often not to scale. Having
traditionally drawn in pencil or pen in a sketchbook
or on pages ripped from a roll of tracing paper,
many designers now think more clearly with
a mouse. These early design drawings should not
be discarded as they can have an important role
in explaining the design 'concept' at a later stage.

Name:
Sketchbook drawing

Location:
N/A

Date:
1999

Designer:
Penelope Haralambidou

The design process > **Thinking drawings** > Drawing to measure

The design process usually begins with a verbal
or written request for a design. This is known
as the brief or programme and can come directly
from the client, or might be in the form of a competition
document or a student assignment. Many clients
will not have great experience of commissioning
a designer and one of the first tasks is to define and
clarify the brief.

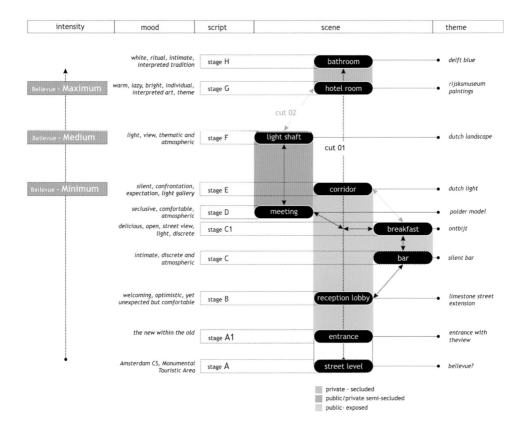

intensity	mood	script	scene	theme
	white, ritual, intimate, interpreted tradition	stage H	bathroom	delft blue
Bellevue - Maximum	warm, lazy, bright, individual, interpreted art, theme	stage G	hotel room	rijsksmuseum paintings
		cut 02		
Bellevue - Medium	light, view, thematic and atmospheric	stage F	light shaft	dutch landscape
			cut 01	
Bellevue - Minimum	silent, confrontation, expectation, light gallery	stage E	corridor	dutch light
	seclusive, comfortable, atmospheric	stage D	meeting	polder model
	delicious, open, street view, light, discrete	stage C1	breakfast	ontbijt
	intimate, discrete and atmospheric	stage C	bar	silent bar
	welcoming, optimistic, yet unexpected but comfortable	stage B	reception lobby	limestone street extension
	the new within the old	stage A1	entrance	entrance with theview
	Amsterdam CS, Monumental Touristic Area	stage A	street level	bellevue?

private - secluded
public/private semi-secluded
public- exposed

Above:
Hotel-o-gram
For this project, Elastik used
schematic form to show
the sequence and routing
of the design process.

'The different stems form a critical
path; the clustering elements
are a relational matrix showing
the dependency between the
intimate and exposed spaces.
It's a movie script.'

Thinking drawings

'Interiors accommodate compositions of programme and activity that change constantly and independently of each other without affecting what is called with accidental profundity, the envelope.'

Rem Koolhaas

Words and image

Name:
Bellevue Hotel

Location:
Amsterdam, The Netherlands

Date:
2005

Designer:
Elastik

Briefs come in many forms – from lists of rooms known as schedules of accommodation, which are very specific – to more open requests such as 'we would like more space'. However it is phrased, form rarely follows neatly behind function and the designer's job is to discuss with the client what they actually want and to come up with solutions. It is not always most useful to immediately come up with formal solutions and first drawings can often look more like bubble diagrams or sequence layouts than plans or perspectives.

When the design firm Elastik were approached to design a 75-bedroom hotel within an existing shell, one of the fundamental requirements was that it should 'show up on the radar'. The client wanted, as much as the beds, a design identity that would attract custom. Elastik responded to the brief by evolving a series of principles and themes on parallel tracks through what they described as a 'hotel-o-gram'. Here, proposed themes, moods, levels of intensity, and definitions of public and private were all juxtaposed to create individual form for each of the spaces within the hotel.

Top left:
Water themed interior

Above:
Grass themed interior
Elastik introduced the three main elements of the Dutch landscape: dunes, grassland and the sea.

Programme brief > Concept board

The term concept board originates from the tradition of interior designers fixing fabric and paint samples and possibly sketches on to a sheet of mount board. Maybe memories of these is why concept boards, or mood boards as they are sometimes referred to, have a slightly dubious reputation. Today, however, concept boards are more likely to be put together in a layout program such as Adobe Photoshop and are widely used in other fields such as marketing and business. Created at the beginning of the design process, they are a method of creating a 'visual conversation' with the client and other members of the design team.

Arrange associate

Name:
House in Notting Hill

Location:
London, England

Date:
2006

Designer:
Emily Pitt

The skill lies both in the arrangement of the parts and the associations made. These can be made more explicit by the use of 'trigger' words such as 'bathe space' or 'eat cook'. The arrangement is, to some extent, proportional so if wood, for instance, is to be the predominant material, it makes sense to give it a strong presence on the sheet. The association is a dialogue between the designer and the client to understand that if one uses the word 'modern' or 'natural,' both parties have the same picture in their head.

In her design for a house in Notting Hill, Emily Pitt used quick sketches and images of examples to discuss with the client various options for a new study area and bathroom. These images were presented alongside text in a document.

Above:
Sample image
Images from sources such as magazines can be used on concept boards to discuss options.

Left:
Sketch of the study
Removing the shower room has the effect of widening the corridor and creating generous space next to the garden.

Below:
Sketch of storage space
The sketch shows potential for a large amount of well-ordered storage space both above and below the desk.

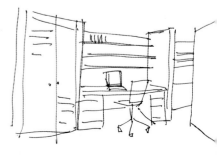

Thinking drawings

Right:
Sample image
Although the sketches
suggest a light colour palette,
image examples taken from
other sources and projects
can show how exaggerating
the darkness of this floor may
be a more interesting approach.

Far right:
Sketch of bathroom
The sketch suggests a new
bathroom on the lower level.

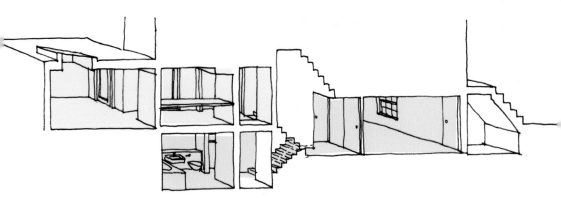

Above:
Section
Colour is used to show use:
green for guest areas and blue
for occupant.

Right:
Sketch of vestibule area
At the foot of the new staircase,
a sort of vestibule area is
created outside the bathroom.

How we use space is far more ambiguous than it might seem at first glance. Form doesn't necessarily follow function and today we recognise interiors are constructed as much by social and cultural customs as physical or formal necessity. Even things that we might take as functional necessities, such the chair, have less importance when one looks to India, China and Japan. It is important, therefore, to look at how a space will be used and how that might potentially change.

Event

Name:
9 Stock Orchard Street

Location:
London, England

Date:
1997

Designer:
Sarah Wigglesworth

Representations of interior space rarely show the space as it will be used in reality. In a study for her project, 9 Stock Orchard Street, Sarah Wigglesworth drew a series of plans of her dinner table to demonstrate how designers should plan space.

Her drawings show a table at three moments in time. Firstly, a perfectly laid dinner table for eight, then as the meal is being eaten and finally as the table is left in disarray after the meal has been eaten. There is nothing extraordinary in this sequence and this is the point. When designers start to draw out how space is to be used they should be realistic about how people actually live, they should represent the chaos and strangeness of everyday life. If it is understood that a living room is also to be used for ballet practice, the designer can design accordingly. The architecture is fixed but an interior is constructed from more mobile elements and, in these early design stages, these should be drawn in all their variations. This does not require complicated drawings – part of the power of 'Table Manners' is the use of the same, simple ink line throughout, signifying such very different things.

'Home is represented not by a house, but by a set of practices. Everyone has his own.'

John Berger

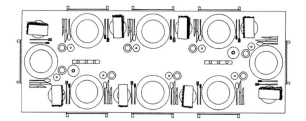

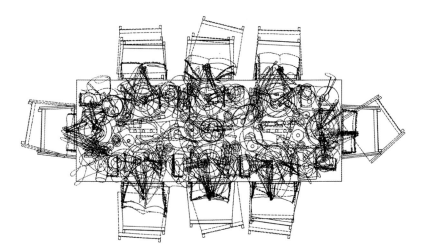

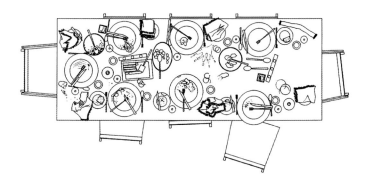

Top to bottom:
Table Manners
Rotring ink line drawings showing the table before, during and after dinner. Sarah Wigglesworth drew these plans to demonstrate how designers should plan space.

'In the action of changing and creating an environment the individual confers meaning on the environment.'

Martin Pawley

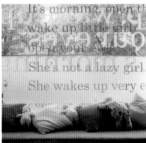

Hybrid space

Name:
Sure Start On The Ocean Children's Centre, Tower Hamlets

Location:
London, England

Date:
2000

Designer:
muf architecture/art

Modern life, particularly in cities, is characterised by a lack of space. The traditional plan showing one function per room has been replaced by plans that show hybrid space and shared use. It is the designer's job to incorporate the differing users into the design.

Architecture and art practice muf uses brief development as an integral part of the creative process. When muf designed an amenity for Sure Start (a British governmental programme delivering childcare and educational services for young children and families), they needed to create a space that could be used by both young children and their adult carers. To do this they created a flexible space that could be immediately transformed between playroom and boardroom, simply by moving the furniture. The glazed façade of Bengali and English texts in gold and scarlet lettering veils views from the street. These texts advertise the work and presence of Sure Start in a way that avoids the usual aesthetic associated with, and the consequent stigma of, community provision.

Above:
Playroom and boardroom
With their flexible design, muf have produced a space that avoids the usual aesthetic associated with community services.

Thinking drawings

Below and bottom:
Plans

Plans showing the playroom
as boardroom (below) and the
boardroom as playroom (bottom).
These drawings cleverly show
how a space can be put to two
very different uses.

Below right:
Multiplan

Moving elements are marked
to show the two types of use
simultaneously.

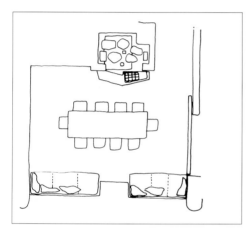

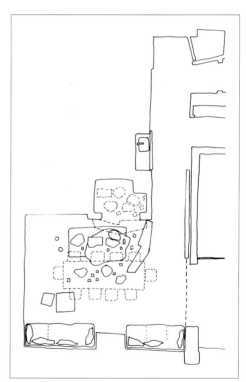

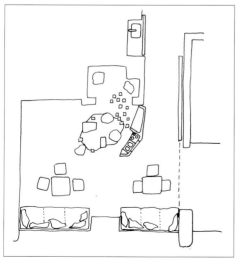

Ever since the architectural critic Sigfried Giedion
established the relationship of space and time in
architecture, designers have been experimenting with
how to represent space, time and movement effectively
in their work. Traditional representation presumes
stable objects and fixed subjects. However, this is often
not the case and this section explores both interiors that
move and how to represent moving through a space.

Right:
Watercolour sketch
Movement is described by dotted
lines, arrows and the inner and
outer surfaces are distinguished
from one another using colour.

Below:
Plan
The plan shows horizontal
movement only.

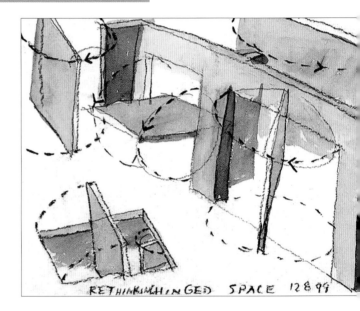

RETHINKINGHINGED SPACE 12899

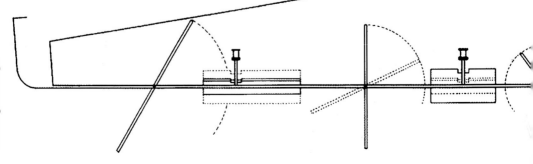

Moving interiors

Name:
Storefront for Art and Architecture

Location:
New York, USA

Date:
1993

Designer:
Steven Holl and Vito Acconci

Interiors are full of moving elements – think of a door, for instance. Moving elements do not require complex drawings. Accepted convention suggests a door is drawn in its open position with an arc tracing its swing back to the frame, thus showing which room it opens into and on which side it is hinged. Dotted lines, arrows and the overlaying of different positions can be used to indicate movement on a plan or section. Other possibilities could include storyboard, flipbooks, choreography, a musical score or a script. These techniques can be used in combination with more architectural drawings.

Steven Holl's façade for the Storefront for Art and Architecture in Manhattan is articulated by a series of hinged panels that open up on to the street. These panels pivot both vertically and horizontally. In his watercolour sketch, Holl is able to describe this movement using dotted lines, arrows and colour to indicate the inner and outer surfaces. It is almost as if the façade is dancing. Plan and section, on the other hand, operate in a single plane and the plan illustrated only shows horizontal movement.

'The interactive dynamic of the gallery argued for an inside-out façade, which addresses insular art and turns it out to the public street. Hinged walls rotate on both axes, which allows some to become tables and benches. The body is linked to the wall forms in the crude way that the shoulder is needed to push space out or pull it in.'

Steven Holl

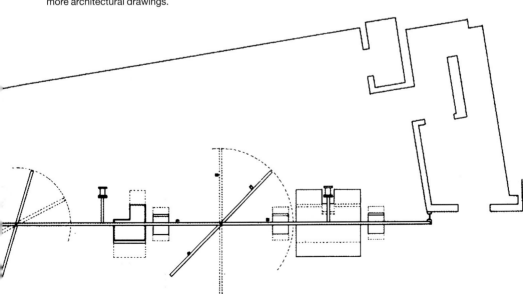

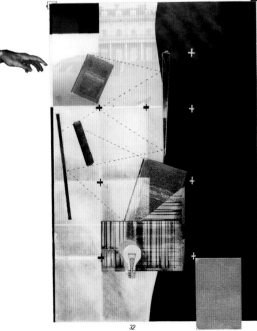

Above:
Interior of gallery
Views through the space
focus on the occupants and
exhibits. This drawing was
made in MicroStation and
Adobe Photoshop.

Right:
Collage
Initial collage exploring the design
concept for the book drop.

Thinking drawings

Movement through space

Name:
Gallery for rare books,
Headington Hall

Location:
Oxford, England

Date:
2007

Designer:
Orit Sarfatti (third-year interior
architecture student at Oxford
Brookes University, England)

'For a building to be motionless is the exception:
our pleasure comes from moving about so as
to make the building move in turn, while we enjoy
all those combinations of its parts. As they vary,
the column turns, depths recede, galleries glide:
a thousand visions escape.'

Paul Valery

The design of interior architecture
should not be seen as a series
of still lifes but rather of spaces
to move around and inhabit.
Unlike a painting or a book,
space is experienced over time
and the designer cannot control
the viewpoint in the same
way a painter or a writer might.
Interiors function more like
a backdrop, slipping in and
out of focus. A designer can
influence the experience to
a certain degree. A suitably
placed bench facing a certain
direction will ensure a view
is enjoyed, for example, or
a carefully placed window at the
end of a corridor will allow natural
light to flood in, arousing curiosity.

The project shown here by Orit
Sarfatti is for a gallery for rare
books. A variety of techniques
were used to explore how the
gallery user moves through the
space, lining up particular views
or moments – some focusing
on the books, some on the space
and some on the view beyond.

Right:
1:1 prototype of mirrored
book drop
A prototype was built to explore
the mirror effect of the book drop.

Below:
Framing the view
Design exhibits slip in and out
of frame as the visitor moves
through the space.

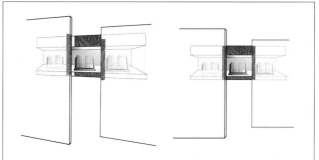

Inspiration can take many forms. It can be conscious or unconscious, implicit or explicit, a generic concept such as 'the sea' or a specific image such as a favourite painting. People in visual disciplines often look to visual images for inspiration but many will also be inspired by non-visual sources such as a piece of music or even an emotion. What is important is the ability of an idea or concept to cross from one medium to another.

Opposite page:
Design model
The second model, inspired by the observations made during the first model-making process.

Above:
Study model
Study model, after Hammershøi's *A woman in an interior*.

Explicit

Name:
Hôtel Project (study model after Hammershøi's *A woman in an interior*)

Location:
Paris, France

Date:
2008

Designer:
Jonathon Connolly (third-year architecture student at London Metropolitan University, England)

The word 'inspire' means to instruct or guide. This process takes many forms. Traditionally, students of architecture would be asked to draw or 'copy' architectural elements such as column capitals as a method of learning the classical orders and proportion. There was a belief that through the act of drawing the principles would be absorbed and learnt. Today the ability to look and learn is still an important part of education and schools of architecture and design often ask students to make this process explicit and show their precedents. What is being examined is not the choice of precedent but the ability to understand and absorb rather than just copy.

In this example a group of students were asked to make a model based on a painting of an interior. The model had to be a 'representation' of the materials depicted in the painting rather than the 'actual' materials. The study model shown here by Jonathon Connolly is constructed of card that has been treated in different ways using chalk, varnish and pastel. The programme then asked for any ideas that were observed during the model-making process to be made explicit in the final design proposition. Thus, the model-making process led Connolly to take the spatial idea of enfilade (an interconnected group of rooms arranged usually in a row with each room opening into the next) from Hammershøi: framing, proportion, and the ability of light to lead the eye and transform surfaces. He went on to develop these ideas in his final proposition. The first model could therefore be called a copy of the painting while the second is inspired by it.

'The difference between a bad artist
and a good one is; the bad artist seems
to copy a great deal. The good one really
does copy a great deal.'

William Blake

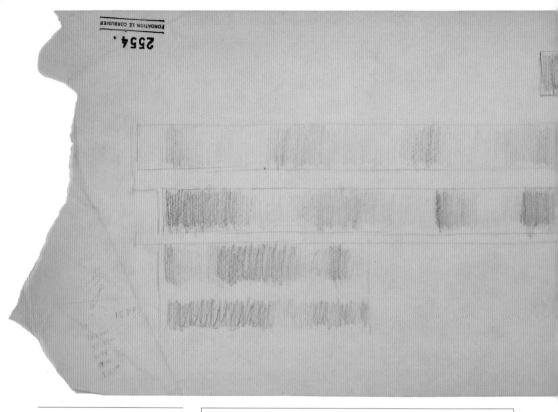

Above:
Study
Early study by Xenakis for
the *pans de verre ondulatoires*,
shown as a band of graded
shading or a 'ruled surface
of sound'.

Right:
Drawing
Drawing showing the rhythm
of the mullions, as built.

'By collapsing the Modular into a line, and by collapsing the intervals along the line into a frequency, he brought something new to architecture.'

Robin Evans

Implicit

Name:
The Priory, La Tourette

Location:
Lyons, France

Date:
1957–1960

Designer:
Iannis Xenakis

Today Iannis Xenakis is best known as a composer. However, he originally trained as an engineer, and between 1948 and 1960 worked as an assistant to the French architect Le Corbusier. In 1953 he was entrusted with much of the design of the Priory of La Tourette, including the *pans de verre ondulatoires* (undulatory glazed panels) used in the refectory. Inspired by the music he was composing and the modular system he had helped to develop with Le Corbusier, Xenakis developed a ribbon of mullions spaced at varying intervals that could be seen as 'three-dimensional music'. The mullions implicitly indicate the rhythm and the glazing bars the tone.

Above:
Glazed panels
The glazing shown in the context of the building.

Sketching is fast, immediate and requires only a pen and paper. Sketches can be drawn on the back of an envelope, in a sketchbook or on a screen. They can be composed of just line or a mixture of line, tone, written notes and collage. Sketches do not have to be works of art but will improve with practice and that is why even in this digital age many designers will always carry a sketchbook. There are two main uses for sketching: firstly as a way of observing and recording and secondly as a way of 'thinking aloud'. The first benefits the second as ideas recorded years before can reappear in the most surprising ways.

Below:
Sketches
Le Corbusier's 1911 sketches of Villa Hadrianus, in particular their depiction of light being reflected down through a curved shaft, were later 'rediscovered' in his design for the Chapel of Notre Dame du Haut in 1954.

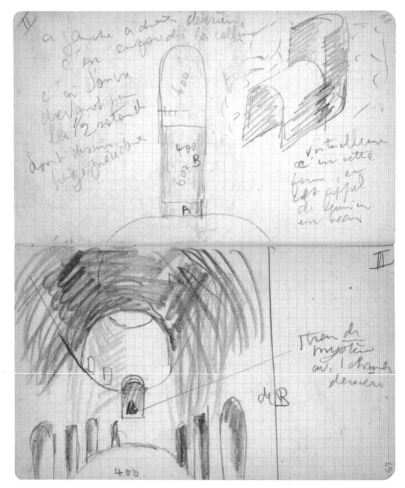

'Cameras get in the way of seeing.'

Le Corbusier

Sketching to observe and remember

Name:
Chapel of Notre Dame du Haut

Location:
Ronchamp, France

Date:
1954

Designer:
Le Corbusier

Many visual artists sketch on their travels. It is well recorded that Le Corbusier always carried a sketchbook around in which he noted down everything that made an impression on him. Often annotated as well as drawn, there is a style to them that suggests a sort of personal shorthand.

Le Corbusier used sketches to record things he felt a camera could not, such as concepts, underlying structure or feelings experienced in a space. Sketching makes one look in a different way and helps form a visual record against an imperfect memory.

Le Corbusier's sketches of Roman Emperor Hadrian's Villa in Tivoli, Italy, record a particular way of bringing light reflected down through a curved shaft of one of the buildings. This quality of light is 'rediscovered' many years later in the side chapel of his church of Notre Dame du Haut at Ronchamp, France, 1954.

Below:
Interior
Inside the towers of the Chapel of Notre Dame du Haut at Ronchamp.

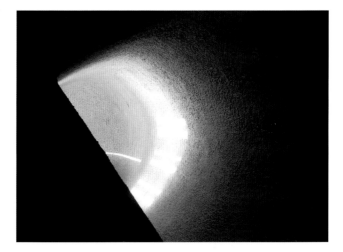

Iconic sketch
Iconic sketches are those enigmatic squiggles of lines that sum up a scheme. The sketches of American architect Frank Gehry might be an example. These type of sketches are deemed of value because they imply a pure process from conception to finished project and come with association of the designer's genius being embedded in their ability to draw. In reality the design process is rarely so straightforward or linear and the iconic sketch is often drawn after the project is completed.

Inspiration > **Sketch** > Diagram

Analytical sketching

Name:
Analytical sketches of Marcel
Duchamp's *Étant donnés*,
Philadelphia Museum of Art

Location:
Philadelphia, USA

Date:
2000 and 2002

Designer:
Penelope Haralambidou

Analytical sketching is when you draw something out in order to understand or explain something to either yourself or others. These types of sketches will include non-formal elements such as lines of sight or measurements, often incorporating fragments of plan, section and perspective on the same page. They could be described as sketching out ideas rather than spaces.

Penelope Haralambidou uses a method of drawing that does not separate the written and drawn elements. Her technique is primarily an investigatory method, a written drawing rather than just a text, line and letter shedding light on the other. Looking rather like a map, the constellation of words connected by lines places ideas spatially, rather than in a linear narrative sequence.

Haralambidou's sketches show a variety of different mediums used to sketch ideas and analytical interpretations of real events and objects.

Below:
Sketch notes in sketchbook
Double spread from a journal of a visit to the Philadelphia Museum of Art to study the hidden interior of Marcel Duchamp's enigmatic *Étant donnés*. She drew in order to analyse both its hidden interior and how the peepholes which allow the viewer to look in control their gaze. Drawn with pencil, ink and Letraline tape.

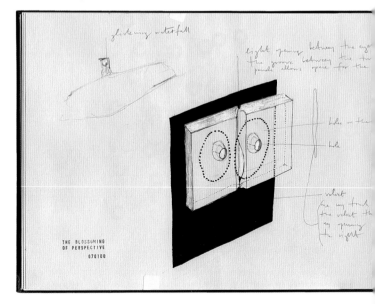

THE BLOSSOMING
OF PERSPECTIVE
070100

Thinking drawings

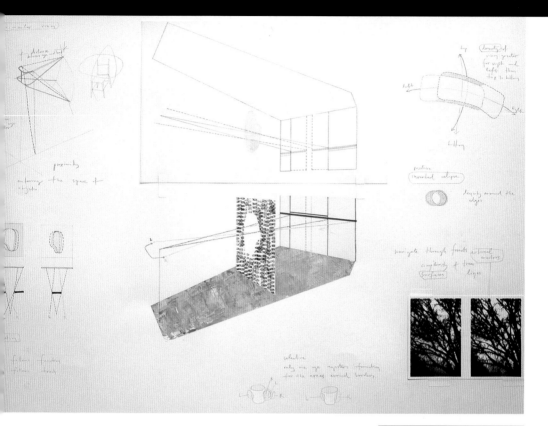

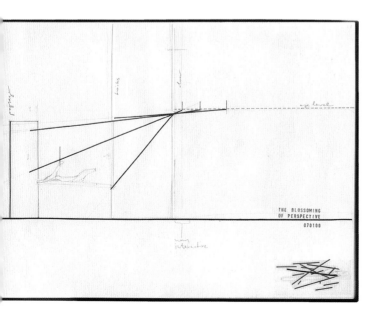

Above:

Drawing of *Étant donnés*

This more complex drawing was constructed at a later date using the drawings and notes from the sketchbook. Using a variety of mediums, Haralambidou describes the interior space more, clearly continuing to analyse the position of the viewer by the use of line. Because of the notes, the collaged elements and diagrams on the sheet, this drawing could still be described as a sketch. Drawn with pencil, ink and Letraline tape on A2 paper.

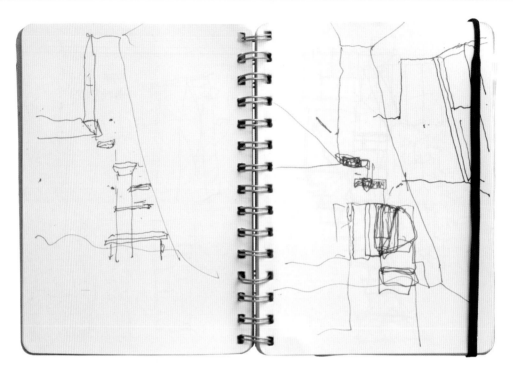

Design sketch

Name:
2 Whatcotts Yard

Location:
London, England

Date:
2005

Designer:
Silvia Ullmayer (Ullmayer
Sylvester Architects)

Sketching to exteriorise
thoughts and ideas is not about
an end product but is an integral
part of the design process itself.
Sketches are an immediate
and intuitive form of drawing.
They are a fast and fluid way
of exteriorising thoughts. The
hand moving across the page,
the eye referring back to the
image in one's head, the line
providing an important tool for
investigating and understanding
potential solutions to problems.
Because of the ease and speed
of sketching they are often done
in a series and it is possible to
literally see the thought process
as it develops.

Thinking drawings

Above and opposite page:
Felt-tip in sketchbook
When it came to adding
a staircase to the suspended
den in 2 Whatcotts Yard,
Silvia Ullmayer literally drew
out the solution; drawing,
looking and modifying the
bespoke steel stair.

Left:
Detail of stair
The finished staircase.

Below:
View through the space
The space into which the
staircase was to be inserted.

Inspiration > **Sketch** > Diagram

Diagrams are abstract drawings that use symbols or ideograms as a graphic shorthand rather than attempting pictorial likeness. Under-used in interior representation, diagrams focus on specific attributes, editing out superfluous information for clarity. This process of editing makes visible or brings to the fore some of the less tangible qualities ignored by other representational techniques and makes comparison between different variations much more clear. Diagrams give the impression of being impervious to style or ideology and can free up the early stages of the design process from the problem of form.

Diagrams can be freehand or measured, described in two dimensions or three and can be drawn in line, tone, or colour. They relate to proportion rather than scale, as they are concerned with relationships of elements rather than being to measure. They should be easily comprehensible and if needed can rely on a simple key or legend. A good diagram can make something complex seem simple and can communicate visually what would take many words. Diagrams tend to be used as either analytical or generative representations.

Analytical or explanatory

Name:
The Archbishopric Museum

Location:
Hamar, Norway

Date:
1979

Designer:
Sverre Fehn

Analytical diagrams resolve or separate a space into its elements or component parts. They can be a way of visualising non-visual information such as circulation or performance. Analytical diagrams can uncover latent structures of organisation and can be used to explain design decisions by separating out functions. Analytical diagrams are ideal for comparisons of an attribute such as variations of the 'cook, wash, store' triangle in the kitchen. They can be used at the beginning of the design process to analyse a particular design issue and they can be used at the end of the process to explain how a space works.

In his design for the Archbishopric Museum in Hamar, Norway, Sverre Fehn devised a 'suspended museum' using series of concrete ramps and walkways that pass through the nineteenth-century barn structure and hover over the medieval excavations without touching the ruins. Aaron Losada's diagram of this very simply explains the three layers of time and construction: the black plan representing the ruins of the old fortress, the grey walls the barn, and the red the new elements that Fehn inserted.

'The fundamental technique and procedure of architectural knowledge has seemingly shifted over the second half of the twentieth century from drawing to diagram.'

Peter Eisenman

Top:
The concrete walkway
Fehn's 'suspended museum' uses a series of walkways and ramps to pass through the old barn and hover above the ancient ruins.

Right:
Exploded diagram
Here, three layers of time and construction are shown: the black plan represents the ruins of the medieval fortress, the grey represents the walls of the nineteenth-century barn and the red represents the new elements that Fehn inserted.

Above:
Watercolour perspective
Watercolour perspective of the proposed space. According to Holl: 'At the building entrance, space curves, vanishing points disappear. Here the figure can be seen in at least three levels due to the upper ramps – the space comes alive with the body-subject. This vast spatial curve is activated from several points of view and several horizons.'

Opposite page:
Diagram
Initial watercolour sketch.

Generative

Name:
Kiasma Museum of
Contemporary Art

Location:
Helsinki, Finland

Date:
1998

Designer:
Steven Holl

Generative diagrams are a conceptual design tool and can be used as a way of thinking in very much the same way as the sketch. They are a technique for visual thinking and problem solving. By freeing the designer from formal decisions they make room for other considerations and allow the designer a more open mind. Peter Eisenman has suggested that the diagram allows designers to analyse the act of design itself. The computer's ability to create drawings in layers that can be isolated means the generative diagram is increasingly being used as a design tool in the early stages of a project.

Steven Holl used diagrams to illustrate his winning proposal for a competition for the design for a Museum of Contemporary Art in Helsinki, Finland. Holl's scheme was code-named 'Chiasma' (meaning a crossing or intersection) and elegantly explored this concept through a 'criss crossing' sequence of spaces.

One of the skills of competition drawing is the ability to explain complex spatial concepts with clear graphics. If one looks at Holl's initial concept diagram one can see him explore the concept of 'intertwining' starting with the simple diagram of two intertwining arrows, developing spatial and formal qualities as the series progresses.

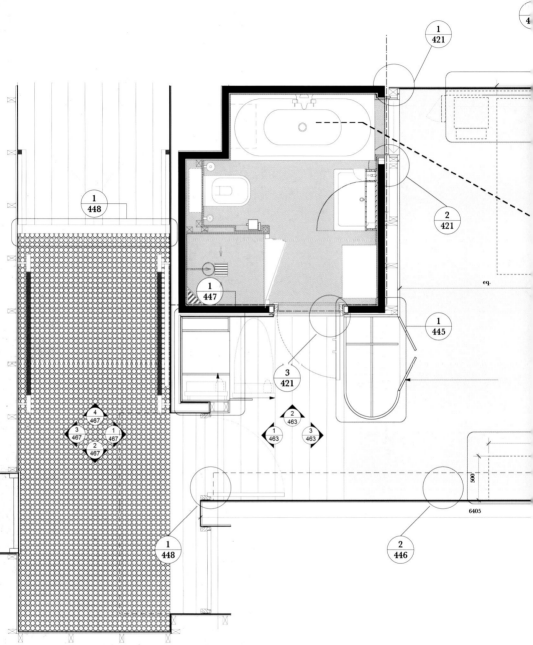

1
421

2
421

1
448

1
447

1
445

2
421

3
421

4
467

3
467

1
467

2
467

2
463

1
463

3
463

eq.

500

6405

1
448

2
446

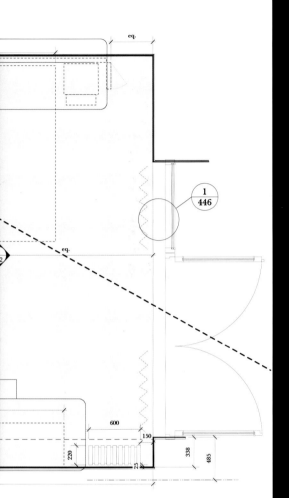

This chapter looks at drawing to measure and scale. Although many other forms of drawing are used, the standard form of drawing buildings is a two-dimensional scaled description of the proposed space cut into a series of orthographic planes known as plan, section and elevation. This is a highly conventionalised, non-pictorial method whose relationship with the proposed/existing reality is through measurement and scale. It is useful professionally as it provides means to quantify the parts, to predict the end result. This section will also look at methods of combining in particular plan and internal elevation with techniques such as the developed surface, axonometric and isometric.

Name:
Standard bedroom plan,
Farnham Estate Hotel

Location:
Cavan, Ireland

Date:
2006

Designer:
Project Orange

People have used scale for millennia, devising systems of transportable measures that often relate to the human body. The Bible tells us Noah's ark was 300 cubits in length, 50 cubits wide and 30 cubits high (the cubit was an ancient measure based on the length of forearm). The metric system is standard in the UK and Europe today – a decimal system of units based on the metre, centimetre and millimetre. Its source of reference is not the body but an arbitrary unit based on the circumference of the world.

Opposite page:
Measurements of the human body from a metric handbook, a type of reference book which gives the dimensions of everything from the body to shelf heights to revolving doors.

Scale and measure

Scale provides a way of drawing a proposal at less than life-size. A scaled drawing is not merely miniature – it has a consistent relation or ratio to the object it refers to. So if one draws at a scale of 1:10, one unit on the drawing represents ten units in the intended space; if working with the metric system, one centimetre will represent ten metres. Because of the sheer size of buildings, scale is a tool that makes it possible not only to fit a drawing on a page but also for the mind to conceive the space as a whole.

Working with scale

As a designer learns to draw they must also learn to think in different scales and to work between them. The ability to project a tiny self into a drawing allows designers to imagine inhabiting the space in front of them and judge the size of things in relation to themselves. Scale can be calculated mathematically but it is much easier to use a converting tool; if drawing by hand this could be a pair of dividers or (more often) a scale rule with different scales marked out on each edge. On a computer most CAD programs draw at full scale, regardless of what size you choose to work at on the screen, the scale of a particular drawing only being fixed when it comes to print.

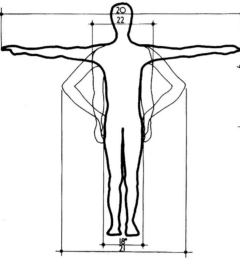

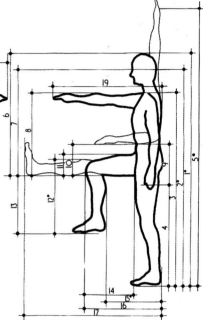

Proportion

There are standard scales used in the industry and one should stick to these: 1:1, 1:5, 1:10, 1:20, 1:50, 1:100, 1:200, 1:500, 1:1250. Graphic convention suggests the designer uses different scales for different types of drawings; as a rule, the smaller the scale the less detail shown. So 1:5 would be for detail, 1:20 for a room and 1:1250 for a city plan. Many drawings that appear later in the book will not be drawn to any scale so are 'not to scale'.

Proportion could be described as the relationship of one thing to another in terms of size. Rather than defining elements by a measurement it describes dimensions in relationship to other dimensions so they are 'proportional' and can be applied at any scale. Thus, a doorway can have the same proportion as a façade but not the same dimensions. Proportions can be simple rules of thumb or complex geometrical constructions. They are associated with aesthetics and underlying rules of nature and beauty. If something is described as 'in proportion' it means it looks right.

Scale and proportion > Orthographic projection

Left:
Blueprint
Architect Clare Cardinal-Pett lying next to blueprints of full-scale details for Louis Sullivan's National Farmers' Bank. The original blueprint is nine feet long and shows details for wood trim in the Consultation Room. The red lines were marked on the drawing by the carpenter.

Full scale

Name:
National Farmers' Bank

Location:
Minnesota, USA

Date:
1908

Designer:
Louis Sullivan

Full scale (also known as 1:1 scale drawing) drawings are drawn at the same size as the intended proposition. The folly of a full-scale drawing of an entire building should be obvious and full-scale drawings tend to be of details, ornament and furniture.

The drawings shown here are original blueprints for the interior of Louis Sullivan's National Farmers' Bank. The image of a person lying next to one gives some idea of their size.

Sullivan would sketch the ornamental designs freehand with a soft pencil at no particular scale. A draftsman would then prepare the full-scale measured drawing. These drawings are working drawings in the true sense of the word, used during the construction of the building by the carpenters, plasterers and other craftsmen.

'Among all the drawings produced by architects, my favorites are working drawings. Working drawings are detailed and objective. Created for the craftsmen who are to give the imagined object a material form, they are free of associative manipulation. They do not try to convince and impress like project drawings. They seem to be saying; this is exactly how it will look.'

Peter Zumthor

Below:
Ceiling detail
A seven-foot-long print of ceiling plaster details, covered with plaster drips and spills. These often became templates for interior elements and the workmen's marks and pinpricks can still be seen. These drawings are usually discarded once the building is complete.

Traditional drawing techniques

Traditionally drawings would have been drawn on cloth. Copies were made by a method of pin-pricking through to the sheet underneath. When tracing paper and film were introduced it was possible to make copies by tracing through tracing paper or by mechanical means such as the blueprint or the photocopy.

Blueprint: An early method of reproducing drawings where the resulting print has a distinctive blue colour and the lines are white.

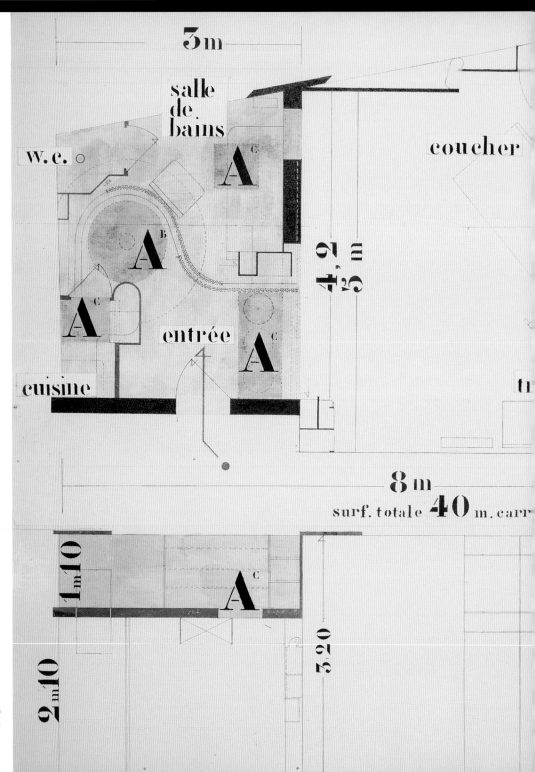

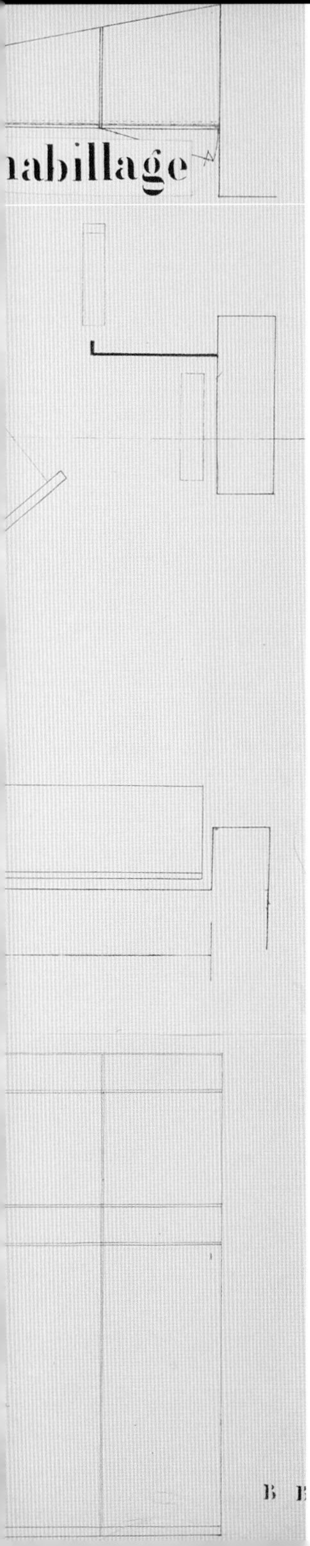

abillage

'Exterior architecture seems to have interested avant-garde architects at the expense of the interior. As though a house ought to be conceived more for the pleasure of the eyes than for the comfort of its inhabitants…'

Eileen Gray

Interior scale

Name:
Jean Badovici's apartment, Rue Chateaubriand

Location:
Paris, France

Date:
1929

Designer:
Eileen Gray

Interior scale mediates between the large scale of the building and the finer, more detailed scale of the body and the object. Generally drawn at scales from 1:5 to 1:50, it is usual to draw the architectural elements and the more mobile furnishings to show how the space is occupied.

In the plan and section shown here, interior architect Eileen Gray describes the layout for an apartment in Paris. The apartment was tiny and the space irregular. Gray's first move was to square the main room by creating a false wall, concealing cupboards and a dressing alcove along the diagonal wall. In the entrance area she provided a tiny kitchenette, bar and bathroom which could be hidden behind a curved metallic curtain, as seen on the plan. In order to minimise clutter she created a false ceiling over the entrance area, shown in grey, designing a series of hidden storage spaces, marked by the letter 'A', that could be reached by a retractable ladder. She notes in her scrapbook, 'in small rooms it is important not to encumber the available space. This can sometimes be realised by mechanical means, obtaining several uses for the same object.'

The section drawn underneath the plan shows how the change in ceiling level also made the main room feel more spacious. The attention to scale and detail blurs the boundary that would let us distinguish what is an architectural element and what is a furniture piece.

Left:
Floor plan and section
Labels indicating the use of different areas such as 'working' or 'dressing' have been pasted on to the plan. Pencil, ink, stencil and ink wash on paper.

Scale and proportion > Orthographic projection

'Maps are a kind of knowledge about the world which offers something by removing something else.'

Kevin Rhowbotham

City scale

Name:
Map of Rome for Pope Benedict XIV

Location:
Rome, Italy

Date:
1748

Designer:
Giovanni Battista Nolli

The interior is not conventionally understood to have an impact at city scale. However, when Giovanni Battista Nolli produced his Map of Rome in 1748 one of the most noticeable features of the map was that the interiors of public buildings such as the Pantheon were represented as part of the city. The map was drawn using a technique known as figure-ground, which means the 'figure' or built areas are hatched to differentiate them from their background. The 'ground', the streets, squares and public interiors, remain white. What is interesting is that the technique reveals these interiors to be as much a part of the city as the architecture that contains them, and in Rome they are understood as public space in the same way as a palace courtyard or one of the many piazzas.

Max Dewdney's Chiaroscuro city explored Nolli's relationship of the interior to the city and developed it in a modern-day context. Working in model, Dewdney explored how the boundaries between what is considered public and private have shifted in Rome. The fragments of models shown refer to specific interiors associated with social and political events that, through media coverage, have become part of the public consciousness despite never having been visited. The project opens up and questions the relationship between actual and psychological space. The technique of using mirror in the models refers to Archizoom Associati's 1970 No-Stop City model, the reflections in the mirrored box making the fragments appear whole, thus creating 'virtual drawings'.

Above:
Map of Rome
Giovanni Battista Nolli's 1748 Map of Rome for Pope Benedict XIV, composed of 12 copper plate engravings, which together measure 176 x 208cm.

Drawing to measure

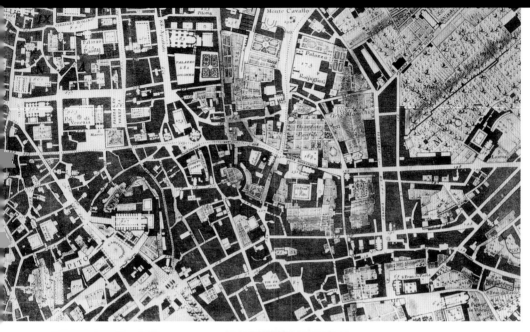

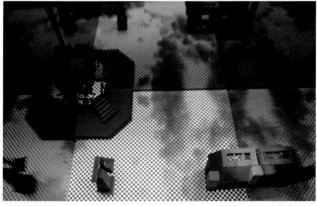

**Left and below left:
Chiaroscuro city**
Max Dewdney's project after
Nolli's Map of Rome uses
fragments of models to refer
to specific interiors associated
with social and political events
that have become part of the
public consciousness, despite
never having been visited.
MDF, black foam-board, painted
wood, shaded mirror, emulsion
paint, 25w red and green light
bulbs, fittings, paper.

Scale and proportion > Orthographic projection

Orthographic projection is a technical term deriving from the Greek *ortho* meaning straight or correct. It refers to a geometrical technique of projecting lines at right angles between a picture plane and an object, usually a building. The projection lines are parallel and the resulting image has no perspective. There are many different types of orthographic projection depending on where you set the picture plane. If it is vertical to the façade of a building the drawing is known as an elevation. However, if the picture plane is set within the building, as if the drawing has cut through like a knife, the view not only cuts through form showing what the building is made of, but also the spaces within. If this cut is horizontal it is known as plan and if it is vertical it is known as section.

Orthographic projection is found in many disciplines, but as a technique it is particularly useful to interior architecture. Plan and section provide a method of opening up the building to look inside. If drawn to scale, different drawings are able to refer to each other and a three-dimensional design can be constructed entirely from two-dimensional drawings.

Right and above right:
Plan and section,
Lauren Skogstad
As part of a design project at Massey University in Wellington, New Zealand, each student was asked to bring a corrugated cardboard box into the studio and explore its interior potential. They had to give their box an entry (door), a view (window) and furnishing. Each box was drawn in relation to site-specific factors in the studio such as electrical outlets, heat, artificial lighting and other boxes. Hand-drawn pastel Conté and graphite.

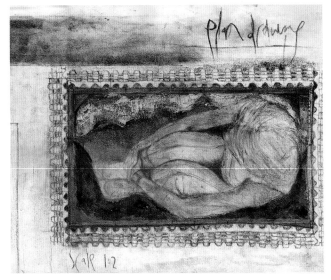

Drawing to measure

'The sign of a truly felt architectural work is that in plan it lacks effect.'

Adolf Loos

Plan, section and elevation

Orthographic projection provides one of the most useful tools available to an interior architect. Abstract in the sense that these drawings do not 'look like' the space they refer to, and flat in that they do not mimic depth, they can seem confusing at first but must be mastered.

Plans and sections are used throughout this book for varying purposes but some general considerations would be: plans are concerned with layout and arrangement; section with space and view. Both can communicate a wealth of information – from what a wall is made of, to positions of doors and windows.

As representational techniques, plans and sections rely on graphic conventions rather than pictorial likeness. These conventions relate to scale, so a section of wall at 1:100 would be drawn as an outline, but at 1:20 the designer would be expected to indicate what material that wall was made of. These codes need to be learned before one starts to experiment.

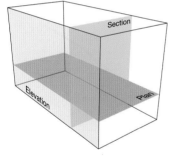

Plan: a horizontal measured cut through a structure, space or object. In buildings the plan is typically cut about a metre above the floor plane looking down or, for a ceiling plan, looking up. A plan can be cut at any desired height for the purpose of design, representation or investigation.

Section: a vertical measured cut through a structure, space or object. The section is generally cut through the centre of the space but again can be cut at any point along the plan.

Elevation: a frontal measured drawing that documents the front face of things. This can be an 'external elevation' or for interior spaces an 'internal elevation'. The edge of an internal elevation also outlines the section of the room.

Scale and proportion > Orthographic projection > Developed surface or unfolded wall plan

The title of this section comes from an essay by the architectural historian and theorist Robin Evans: *The Developed Surface: an Enquiry into the Brief Life of an Eighteenth-Century Drawing Technique*. In the essay he describes an eighteenth-century technique for describing interior space where the five discontinuous planes of a room are folded out and placed on the singular plane of the drawing. 'It became a way of turning architecture inside out, so that internal rather than external elevations were shown.' No outside, not even wall thickness, is drawn so as a technique it shows more 'interior' and less of everything else.

Original techniques

Name:
Hall, Harewood House

Location:
Yorkshire, England

Date:
1771

Designer:
Robert Adam

Developed surface is an interesting method of working as it is quick to comprehend, accurate to scale and it operates as both drawing and maquette in one. It can be a fast route to proposition. If the brief requires a new interior in an existing building, developed surface provides a method of inserting one model into another, clarifying the relationship of the 'inside of the outside' and the 'outside of the inside', reminding all that there can be a space in between. Developed surface is a flat drawing technique that puts focus on surface, notably the walls, but its obvious limitations in describing other qualities such as furniture arrangement resulted in the technique falling out of fashion by the beginning of the twentieth century.

Developed surface

Adam's developed surface
for the hall at Harewood House
puts emphasis on the surface,
notably the walls.

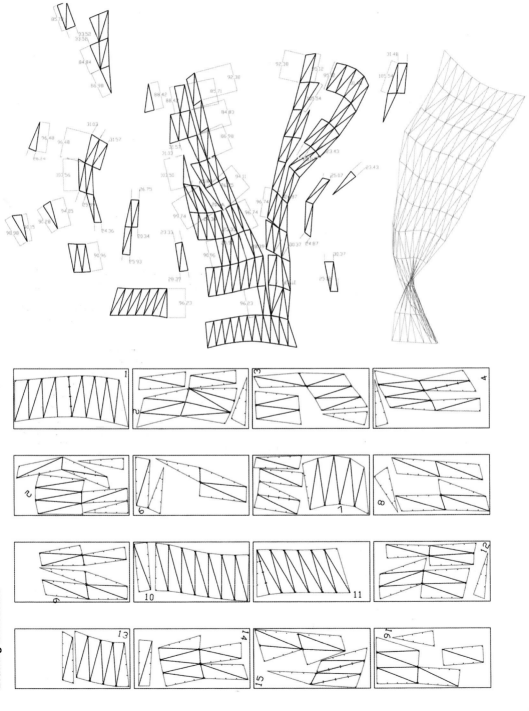

'Imagine a room where a floor becomes wall becomes ceiling becomes wall, and floor again… room loops the loop.'

Rem Koolhaas

New techniques

Name:
California: stage set for John Jasperse

Location:
Various

Date:
2003

Designer:
Ammar Eloueini

New digital technologies have given developed surface a new impetus. In particular the laser cutter uses orthographic drawings created on CAD to direct the output of a laser beam on flat sheet materials, which it can either cut or emboss. Using this technique, there is a direct relationship between the drawing and the finished object. The flat drawings are constructed like a dressmaker's pattern, which when assembled can model complex spatial arrangements. No longer confined to walls, the technique is being developed for use in furniture design, stage sets or other such objects.

New impetus also comes from a growing interest in 'folding' as a generative process in design studios. New software running folding algorithms means folding is seen as a generative design tool rather than just a graphic technique. The complex folded surfaces created by such software break down barriers between inside and outside and redefine where floors end and walls begin, everything becoming a continuous surface. As such, an eighteenth-century drawing technique developed to depict the surface of the walls of a room has evolved into a tool for spatial generation.

Top and above:
Live performance
The set consisted of a mobile canopy created from 34 polycarbonate panels held together with plastic zip ties that the performers can manipulate at will.

Opposite page:
Drawing of stage set
Employing software normally used for fabric applications, the geometric composition was unfolded, parsed into flat interlocking triangles that were then scored, cut and reassembled in translucent polycarbonate using CNC technology.

Axonometric, also known as 'paraline', is constructed by placing a plan at 45 degrees to the paper edge and extruding or projecting the edge lines vertically to describe the walls. Isometric works on the same principle but the plan is set at 30 degrees. The attraction of axonometric lies in its ability to offer a swift method of constructing a three-dimensional view while allowing for 'true' measurements in all three dimensions. However, the resulting interior will have no perspective because the projecting lines are parallel, and the image can look distorted with the viewer placed floating above or below the space. As a rule axonometrics suit more rectangular designs.

Opposite page:
Axonometric drawing
Choisy's drawings showed buildings as the eye could never see them – sliced open and from below, combining plan, section, and interior space in a single view.

Axonometric

Name:
Hagia Sophia

Location:
Istanbul, Turkey

Date:
1899

Designer:
Auguste Choisy

Axonometric is not as modern as it might seem. The technique is commonly found in traditional Chinese and Japanese narrative scroll paintings to depict interior spaces constructed from sliding walls, painted screens and tatami. Its ability to objectively measure and predict form means axonometric drawing was used by the military and engineers, and its development is associated with mechanisation and industrialisation.

During the twentieth century, axonometric was adopted by the modernist avant-garde such as the supremacists because of its abstract diagrammatic-like qualities that had no associations with the illusionistic pictorial world that had come before.

Axonometric is seen as a useful drawing technique for the interior because of its ability to depict interior space. However, the axonometric view is from 'outside the box' and in order to show the interior, designers use a variety of conventions, such as the removal of a ceiling or wall, or a dotted line giving an x-ray effect. Another possibility is the technique used by the architectural historian Auguste Choisy in his *Histoire d'Architecture* in 1899. He drew the illustrations from below with what is sometimes referred to as 'worm's eye' view. This technique allowed him to draw three orthographic planes – plan, section, elevation – and explain the structure in one image.

Integral to this type of axonometric is the description of the internal space, in particular the ceiling with all its domes and vaults. As Cesar Daly, a contemporary reviewer, pointed out in 1874, it was, 'A system that offers the advantage of providing measurements as well as the depiction.'

Drawing to measure

'Axonometric projection, originating in the abstract
and instrumental world of the technical disciplines,
does not map vision. It is concerned instead
with construction and consistency of measurement.'

Stan Allen

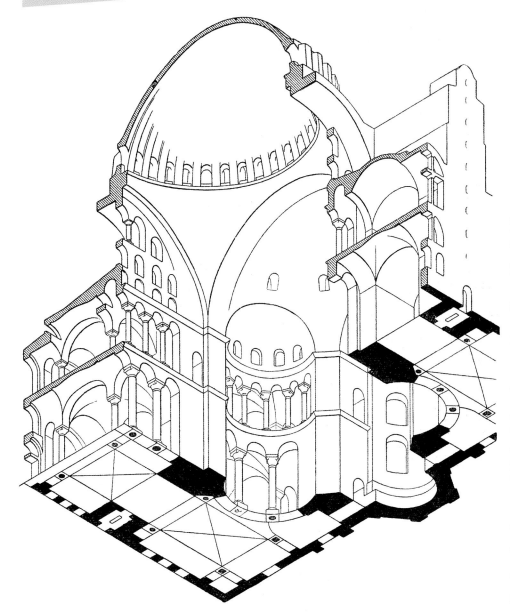

Developed surface or unfolded wall plan > **Axonometric and isometric** > Detail

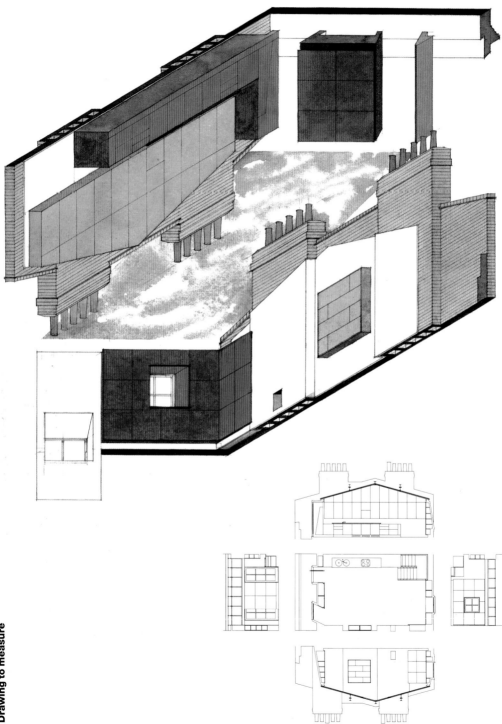

'Delight in colour was developed earlier than delight in form.'

Gottfried Semper

Isometric

Name:
L House

Location:
London, England

Date:
1990

Designer:
Sauerbruch Hutton Architects

In a project known as the 'L House' Sauerbruch Hutton Architects converted a Victorian house to contain two floors of office space and a maisonette above. It was the first of their built projects to which they applied colour in the same way as one would a building material. As one passes up through the house from one storey to the next the intensity of the colour increases, such that the uppermost room appears to be made entirely of colour, creating an ambiguity between the visual and physical enclosure. The glass ceiling open to the sky provides a changeable setting, the weather continuously redefining the mood of the room.

Colour is perceived as relative to other colours around it and this isometric solves the problem of being able to see all sides of the box by placing half the room upside down, connected only at the glass ceiling. This visual distortion gives an effect not unlike lying on your back on the floor. Both the isometric and the developed surface on the opposite page are to scale.

Opposite page top:
Watercolour isometric
This was the first of Sauerbruch Hutton's built projects where colour was applied as an actual building material. Simultaneously enclosing and releasing the space, the colour creates an ambiguity between visual and physical enclosure.

Opposite page bottom:
Developed surface of top floor plan and elevations
The space shown as a developed surface. This technique does not allow the viewer to feel they are in the space.

Above:
Inside the space
The glass ceiling open to the sky provides a changeable setting.

Detail drawing, as the name suggests, is the drawing of elements of a proposal at a detailed or large scale (1:1, 1:2, 1:5) in order to explore and explain how different materials fit together. Like anatomical drawings, details reveal the secrets of construction, the art of joining and the hidden geometries that are not apparent in the completed proposal. Because of this they are usually drawn with orthographic techniques that cut and reveal, such as plan, section or exploded axonometric.

Detail on scale of body

Name:
Piamio Sanitorium

Location:
Piamio, Finland

Date:
1933

Designer:
Alvar Aalto

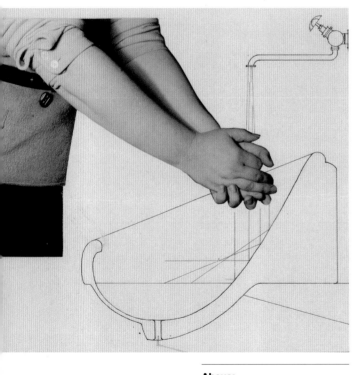

'The main purpose of the building is to function as a medical instrument… one of the basic prerequisites for healing is to provide complete peace… The room design is determined by the depleted strength of the patient, reclining in his bed. The colour of the ceiling is chosen for quietness, the light sources are outside the patient's field of vision, the heating is orientated to the patient's feet and the water runs soundlessly from the taps to make sure no patient disturbs his neighbour.'

The above quote from the Finnish architect Alvar Aalto reveals the intent behind the detailing for Piamio Sanatorium. The surface of the washbasin shown is carefully angled to silence running water as it falls into the basin below: Aalto is not just detailing a washbasin but also a general atmosphere of peace for the patient. The smallest detail affects the whole.

Above:
Section through washbasin
Ink, pencil, and photo collage on board, describing the detail of the washbasins.

Drawing to measure

'The details establish the formal rhythm, the building's finely fractionated scale. Details when they are successful are not mere decoration. They do not distract or entertain. They lead to an understanding of the whole of which they are an inherent part.'

Peter Zumthor

Above:
Photograph of washbasin
Aalto wanted to create washbasins that would allow water to run soundlessly, thus maintaining a calm and peaceful atmosphere for patients at the Piamio Sanitorium.

Constructing a detail

To draw details requires knowledge of materials, their dimensions and how elements come together, and this can make them intimidating drawings for a student. However, once it is understood that drawing a detail is as much about research and an understanding of the desired end effect as it is about the actual act of drawing, details can become one of the most poetic and enjoyable types of drawing.

Detail drawings can be drawn on a computer, with a ruler, or freehand. Some of the best details are drawn with a blunt pencil on the back of an envelope in response to an issue on site. There are graphic conventions to indicate materials and it is usual to use text as well as graphic. The text both confirms drawn elements (for example, 'countertop 50mm timber') and describes things that are difficult to draw (for example 'with rounded pencil edge'). It must be clear which graphic the text is referring to. The detail should always refer back to the bigger picture and be able to be located on an overall plan or section. There are various conventions for this and people have a style of detailing.

Axonometric and isometric > **Detail** > Survey drawing

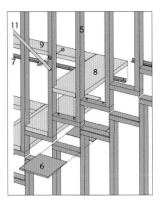

**Above and right:
Drawing of staircase**
Dotted lines show how the
elements fit together.

1
Ground floor

2
External walls below ground level

3
External walls above ground level

4
Landings

5
Studwork spine

6
Packers

7
Wall angle brackets

8
Stair treads

9
Shelves

10
Alternate stair tread from
second floor to utility area

11
Handrails

12
Front door

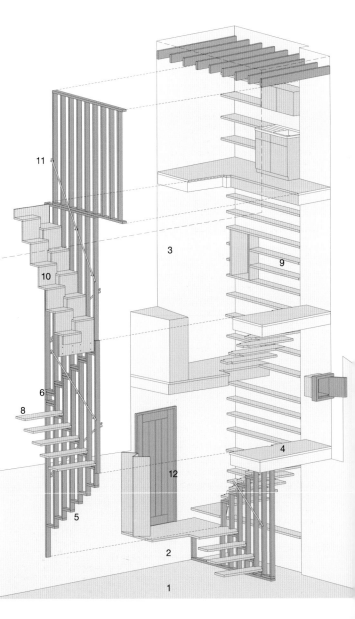

Drawing to measure

'Detailing, the act of drawing one component in relationship to another, forces us to consider how the elements of a building will work together, what effect one has on the others.'

Graham Bizley

Detail on scale of interior

Name:
Newington Green House staircase

Location:
London, England

Date:
2005

Designer:
Prewett Bizley Architects

Newington Green House sits on a tight urban site with space at a premium. The staircase organises the interior, acting as both a transitional element between levels and activities and as storage for the bits and pieces associated with those activities.

Inspired by John Soane's staircase at Lincoln's Inn, this staircase is designed to be a space to pause and occupy rather than just pass through and is lined with bookcases and hidden cupboards. Starting with shoes, coats and bicycles at street level, it progresses to shelves for CDs, then books, then laundry by the bathroom and finally a garden shed opening on to the roof terrace. As an additional design requirement, the owner of the property constructed the stair himself so it had to be made with simple joints using prefabricated elements that were cut down on site to fit.

As can be seen from the drawings, the stair starts out as a sketch and is then developed into a kit of parts. The stair treads change as the stair progresses, but the language of the detail and materials means the staircase is read as a whole.

Below:
Initial concept sketch
The sketch shows the route taken by the staircase through the building.

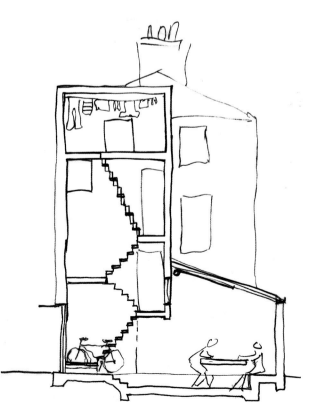

Axonometric and isometric > **Detail** > Survey drawing

'The joint, that is the fertile detail, is the place where both the construction and the construing of architecture take place.'

Marco Frascari

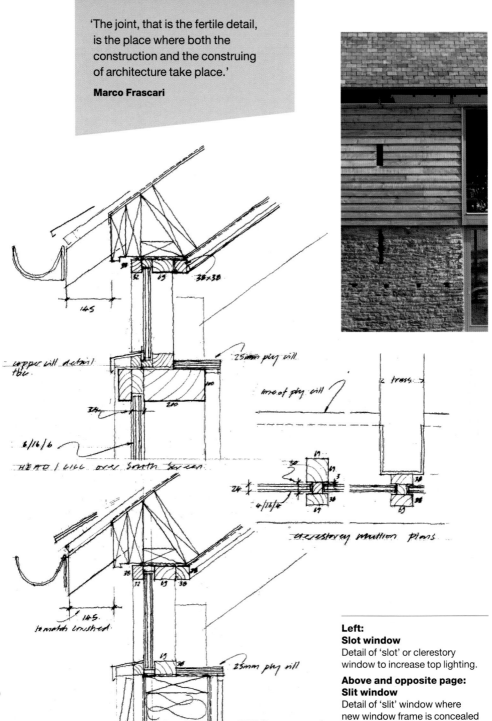

Left:
Slot window
Detail of 'slot' or clerestory window to increase top lighting.

Above and opposite page:
Slit window
Detail of 'slit' window where new window frame is concealed behind clapboard.

Detail on scale of exterior

Name:
New offices

Location:
Hereford, England

Date:
2006

Designer:
Architype

When Architype converted
an existing derelict agricultural
building in Hereford into their
offices they had to alter the
exterior to make the interior
functional for its new use. With
sustainability top of the agenda,
the first task was to increase
natural light and ventilation levels
to create a suitable workspace
environment. They devised
a system of slits and slots
that picked up on the existing
'language' of the old barn on the
outside while providing a bright
modern interior on the inside.

When working with old buildings
elements are rarely square,
straight and to measure. These
drawings are freehand, in pencil
and, although at scale, have key
dimensions written on to them.
The builder has to work between
the drawing and the building,
checking dimensions on site
as indicated by notes such as
'to match cowshed'. Working
drawings such as these are
created in packages with a legend
at the bottom of the sheet as
a method of referring drawings
against each other by date
and issue number. A note known
as a revision is added if any
changes are made.

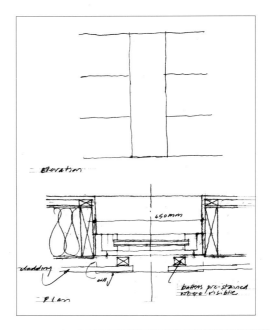

Questions to consider when drawing a detail

Asking the following questions can help when the
interior architect is faced with a choice of solutions:

What overall effect is one trying to achieve? Details
are usually drawn at small-scale (1:5, 1:1, for example)
but their effect will be at the large scale. Details provide
the character of a space.

Is the detail generic? This means is it repeated
and reworked over the design, or is it in response
to a particular activity? The smallest detail can
have a huge impact on the whole if it is generic.

Are the materials chosen suitable for the task?
How will they age or wear? How does it look against
other solutions in the proposal?

How energy-efficient is it?

Who is going to make it?

Axonometric and isometric > **Detail** > Survey drawing

Interior architects will often find themselves working within existing buildings and spaces. Some of the first drawings to be made for a proposal will therefore be a survey or record of the building in its existing condition. The more accurate and thorough the survey the easier the subsequent work will be.

Survey drawing and recording

Name:
Heide II

Location:
Victoria, Australia

Date:
1967

Designer:
McGlashan Everist

The job of the survey drawing is to record all the information that might be useful or inform the proposed design. Survey drawings should therefore include information that is not recorded in conventional plan and section: materials, construction details, the 'language' of the building and views into the space.

A camera can be a useful tool to give a visual record of a space, lighting conditions and colours. Because initial survey drawings are drawn while visiting the site, they will often be quick, rough and in the form of sketches and notes, with layers of information and use of colour to highlight important aspects. These can be tidied up and added to back at the studio.

First check if the original plans and sections exist. It is important to establish at which scale they are drawn; they could be in imperial scale (feet and inches) or a photocopy and no longer at any scale. The drawings should be checked that they are 'as built' and any alterations that have occurred to the building should be noted.

Heide II in Victoria, Australia was designed by McGlashan Everist as a home for John and Sunday Reed. Today it forms part of the Museum of Modern Art. The building is formed by a collection of planar elements that appear to be sliding past each other, a spatial configuration in plan that is not dissimilar to a De Stijl painting. There are no internal doors. Spatial separation is achieved through the extension of walls concealing openings. Overlapping walls restrict views through to adjacent spaces. The effect of moving through the interior is one of unfolding. Roger Kemp of RMIT drew the interior of Heide II, exploring methods that could record its interior qualities, its spatiality and views through. These drawings were initial drawings made whilst in the Heide II. Each drawing is made from a specific location in the space and this is recorded on the plan with added annotation below.

'Unlike many other design- and art-based disciplines, which often begin with the theoretical stance of the artist, the design of the interior is always influenced by the experience of the place that it is to inhabit.'

Graeme Brooker and Sally Stone

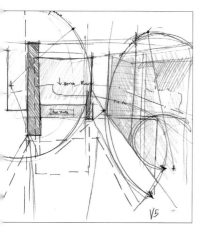

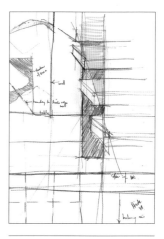

Above:
View 5

Standing in the double-height space, there is an expanse of glass to the right that allows views into the courtyard. Here we are looking at the back wall, which is solid limestone. There is a narrow window to the left. This window runs up past the mezzanine floor to the space beyond.

The circular lines speculate on the expanse of the tree canopies outside given the view through both windows. The crosses give location to the base of the trees. A curved line indicates the walking track that winds its way around the building outside. The Yarra river is envisaged to be somewhere beyond the back wall of the space and is indicated as another broken line.

Above:
View 7

Standing on the mezzanine looking across to the top of the stairs, there is a gap between two walls. This offers a narrow, vertically oriented framed view through to the courtyard. This continues to be seen through the open spaces between the stair treads. The yellow rendered blocks indicate the composition of gaps seen between the staircase. A plan drawing indicates my location on the mezzanine.

Above:
View 8

Standing on the mezzanine looking across to the stairs and the glazed wall. The view extends to the courtyard beyond the double-height space.

The gap articulated in the previous drawing is again presented in this drawing. The shadows of the trees are outlined together with the courtyard walls. Dotted lines indicate a table located in the space. An arrow indicates the position of the mezzanine.

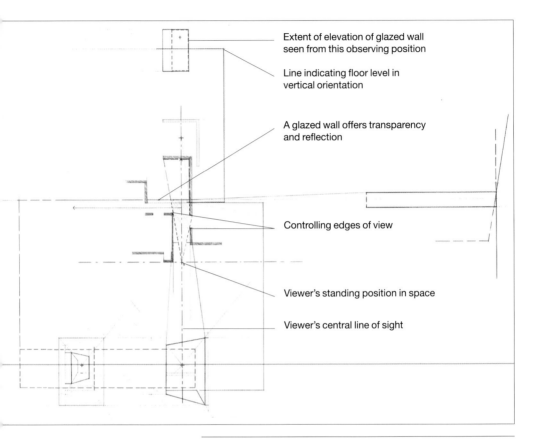

Extent of elevation of glazed wall
seen from this observing position

Line indicating floor level in
vertical orientation

A glazed wall offers transparency
and reflection

Controlling edges of view

Viewer's standing position in space

Viewer's central line of sight

**Above and opposite page:
Plans**

These drawings were made back
in the studio and refer to the
previous ones (the existing plans,
sections and photographs). They
are predominantly plan drawings
recording the viewer's position
relative to what they can see.

They use fragments of section,
perspective and annotation to
describe relationships betweeen
parts of the drawing. The
drawings work as a sequence
of stopping, assessing location
by looking through the existing
space and then moving forward
to the next position for another
assessment of location.

'It is my contention that a conventional set of existing drawings is not able to document space from an interior point of view… this method of drawing literally removes a point of view. The ultimate effect is to remove the viewer from a space.'

Roger Kemp

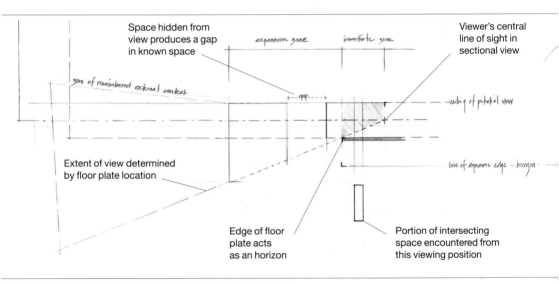

Space hidden from view produces a gap in known space

Viewer's central line of sight in sectional view

expansion zone

investute zone

zone of remembered external context

↞-- app ---↠

ceiling of potential view

Extent of view determined by floor plate location

line of apparent edge - horizon -

Edge of floor plate acts as an horizon

Portion of intersecting space encountered from this viewing position

Checklist of things to note on a survey drawing

Context: immediate, local, historical, wider?

Access: thresholds, boundaries, public, private?

Structure: what is structural? what can be altered?

Services: water, electrical, gas?

Materials: what? where? pattern, rhythms, scales?

Space: levels, arrangement, movement through, solids, voids?

Orientation: sun, wind, light/shade?

Views: inside/outside, point of view?

Detail » Survey drawing

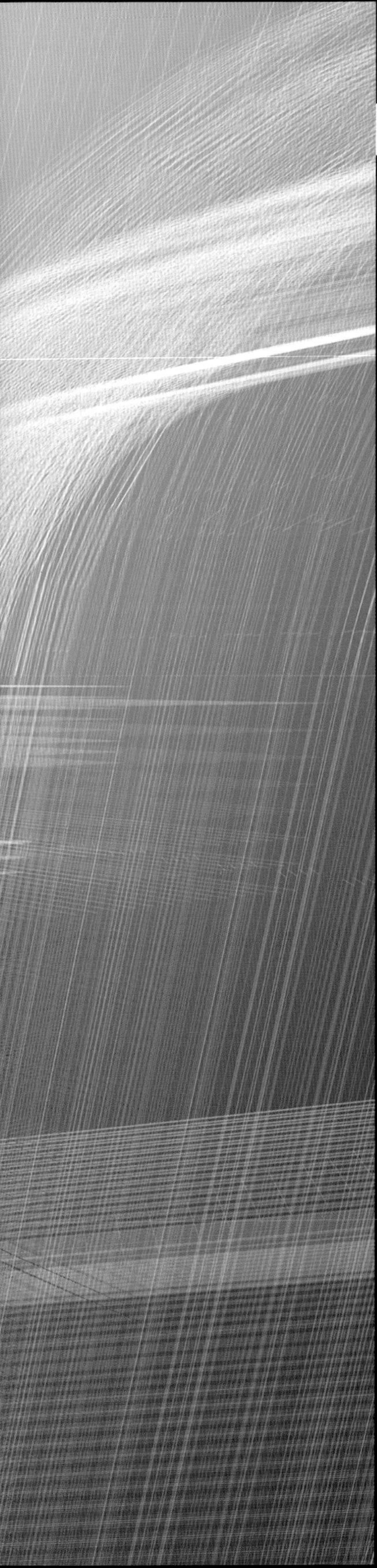

The previous chapter described how to draw
form using orthographic projection. This chapter
is concerned with how to draw the space the
form contains. Space does not register in plan
and section and the interior architect, far
more than the architect, will work in the third
dimension. Three-dimensional drawings and
models provide simulations of a proposition,
as the eye would see it. Traditionally this would
be via a hand-drawn perspective or physical model
constructed from plans and sections. Today,
however, the computer, with its ability to describe
complex three-dimensional geometry
in virtual space, has revolutionised the design
process. The introduction of CADCAM tools
is blurring the boundary between what is
understood as two or three dimensions and
many designers now start the design process
by constructing a three-dimensional digital
model, only later generating plan and section.

Name:
At Play
Location:
N/A
Date:
2004
Designer:
Victoria Watson

The word perspective comes from the Latin *perspicere*: to see through. The easiest way to understand perspective is if one thinks of a piece of glass inserted between the designer and the object they wish to draw. The image is then traced on the glass. Unlike orthographic projection where the lines of projection are parallel, in perspective drawing the lines of projection converge on the viewpoint (the viewer's or painter's eye) and thereby give an illusion of depth. Although it is often described as 'realistic', linear perspective should be understood as a visual convention, unique to European art. Due to its widespread use, however, it has become universally accepted as the primary method of depicting space.

Right:
Seeing space
Benayoun's panorama digitally maps the gaze of viewers as they move around a gallery site in Avignon.

Ways of seeing

Name:
Art Impact, Collective Retinal Memory

Location:
Avignon, France

Date:
2000

Designer:
Maurice Benayoun

'We never look at just one thing: we are always looking at the relation between things and ourselves. Our vision is continually active, continually moving, continually holding things in a circle around itself, constituting what is present to us as we are.' (John Berger, 1990). As we wander through and experience an interior our eyes are constantly in motion, roving over and around the space. Through this constant scanning we form a picture in our 'mind's eye'. This picture is not a single image but layers of images, constructed as much by how we have been taught to see, as by what we actually see.

Because of the complexity of this image we will never represent how we see. However, there are various techniques shown in this section and different designers discuss their preferences. Whatever the method, many designers and particularly students find working in three dimensions to be much more spontaneous and creative than the more abstract orthographic drawings. Because they 'look like' the proposal they are more accessible and understandable to lay people. Be warned, however, because they can also be more deceptive!

Using perspective

Name:
Study after Vermeer's
The Love Letter

Location:
N/A

Date:
2001

Designer:
Philip Steadman

Orthographic drawings give
the designer an abstract slice
through the whole space.
Perspective offers quite a different
view. In the drawings shown here,
Philip Steadman reconstructs
the perspectival space of the
painting *The Love Letter* by
seventeenth-century Dutch artist
Vermeer, in plan, section and
axonometric. The drawings show
how little of the room is actually
'in the picture'. This is because
unless one puts the spectator
outside of the space or accepts
a very distorted angle of vision
perspective only draws part
of the space.

So what is perspective for?
Perspective allows the viewer
to stand in the space in a way
the drawings discussed in the
previous chapter (including
axonometric) never can. It is
about focal points in a room
and the arrangement of elements
and furniture. It can show the
relationship of five surfaces: three
walls, the floor and the ceiling
and their openings (that is doors
and windows). Perspective
can be useful to show the more
experiential qualities of the interior
such as the space itself, light
qualities and views beyond.
Many designers use perspective
as much to test ideas for
themselves as to show a client.

If constructed correctly
perspective can be true to
measure. Although Vermeer's
house no longer exists Steadman
was able to reconstruct the
geometry of the room and
all the furniture in it with great
precision from the painting,
using the floor tiles and objects
that still exist today as reference
points. A measured perspective
can be extremely beautiful but
also time consuming so take care
to select the right view.

Above:
Axonometric
Using the the floor tiles and
objects that still exist in Vermeer's
house, Philip Steadman was
able to reconstruct the geometry
of the room in which the painting
was made.

Opposite page:
Plan and elevation
These drawings show how little
of the room is actually shown in
Vermeer's painting.

Right:
Artist's viewpoint
This diagram shows the diagonal
lines (created by the pattern
of the floor tiles) converge to
a distance point on the horizon.

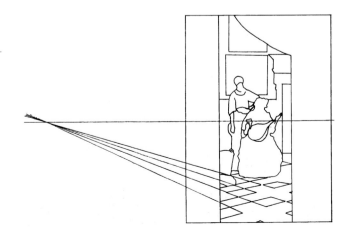

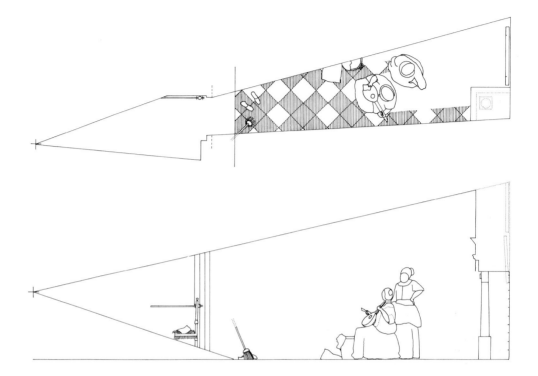

Terms used in perspective

Foreshortening: linear perspective traces lines of projection from a perceived object to a viewpoint, usually the spectator's eye. The width and height of the object decreases as the object recedes.

Overlapping, size and position: overlap works on the idea that if a portion of one object in the field of view is hidden by another, the viewer assumes one is in front of the other. This, combined with the visual understanding that something larger is nearer, means that perspectival images can be constructed by the relationship of elements rather than tracing lines back to a vanishing point.

Shading: addition of a light source will cast shadows and give depth. To prevent the space becoming too dramatic multiple light sources can be used.

Focus: objects that are in focus attract the eye's attention. Usually this will be the foreground, the background being drawn lighter and out of focus.

Perspective effects

Name:
Proposals for Row House and
Museum for a Small City

Location:
N/A

Date:
1931 and 1942

Designer:
Mies van der Rohe

The architect Mies van der Rohe used perspective rather than axonometric to draw space. A skilled draftsman and accomplished at conventional linear perspective and orthographic techniques, Mies developed a personal perspectival language introducing collaged elements. Some of his later drawings were constructed entirely by collage with no lines. The architecture plays a secondary role of framing the views and in some cases is entirely absent.

So what was Mies trying to do? The interiors by Mies that survive today could be described as modernist and minimal but also attract increasing interest for their use of material and effect. The drawings illustrated are for unrealised projects but seem to be testing these qualities, putting the viewer into the space, exploring the relationship between elements and their materiality, even using real materials on the page such as wood veneer.

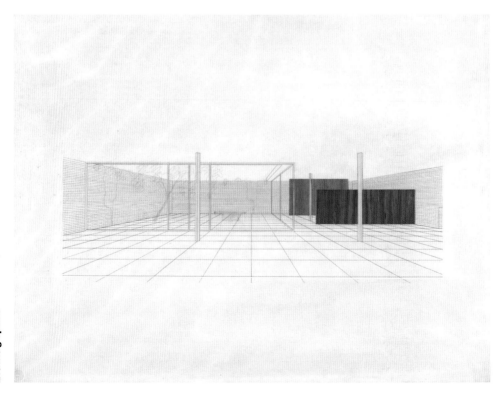

Opposite page:
Interior perspective,
Row House
The receding lines on the floor
tiles indicate a single point
perspective; overlapping
indicates the darker veneered
object is in front of the lighter
one. Pencil and wood veneer
on illustration board.

Below:
Interior perspective,
Museum for a Small City
Cutout reproductions on
illustration board. If one looks
at this image one reads it as art
pieces in a gallery with a window
behind. However, there are no
other clues to this apart from
overlapping and strips cut out
of the 'windows', indicating
mullions. The architecture
is present only in its absence,
the space constructed through
its interior elements.

Above:
Physical model
Physical model of Airgrid made with lustrous coloured thread sewn/drawn into foam board armature.

Right:
Early grid drawings, 2000
Ink, pencil, tracing paper, inkjet transparency.

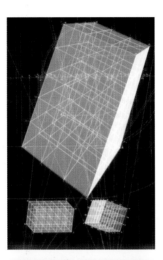

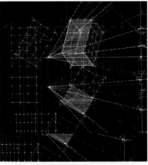

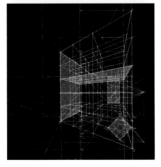

Perspective space

Name:
New Airgrid, after Mies van der Rohe's National Gallery

Location:
Berlin, Germany

Date:
2002

Designer:
Victoria Watson

Mies van der Rohe explored the construction of space rather than form in his perspective collages, describing a set of relations in space rather than the architecture itself.

As part of her PhD research, Victoria Watson developed this idea, using her experience of his buildings to inspire and develop a method of drawing space that she calls 'Airgrid'. Watson focused not so much on what the buildings look like but rather the experiences that they evoke in the visitor. She particularly looked at Mies' use of the grid, which underlies many of his designs without being expressed in the final form.

It is the presence of this grid that gives Miesian spaces the quality of weightlessness she was interested in. Early models of the implied grid were constructed in coloured thread with elements suspended within. Later models develop this technique further, such as those shown here depicting the New National Gallery in Berlin.

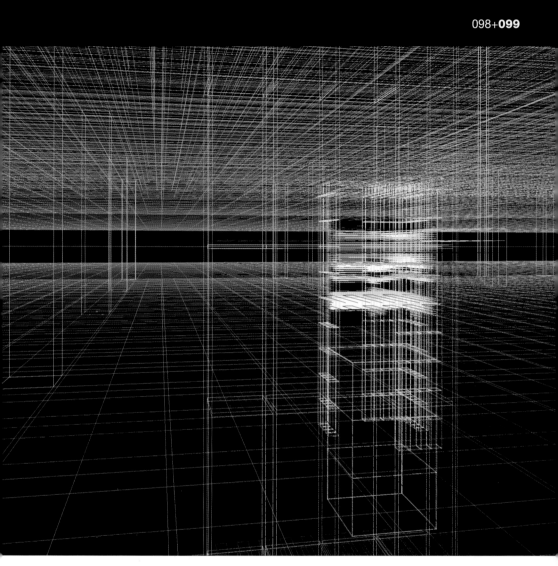

Above:
Digital model, 2002
Digital model of interior of the
New National Gallery. Through
her models, Victoria Watson
focused on the experiences
evoked by the interior, not what
the interior looked like.

Perspective > Physical model

The word model can mean both a three-dimensional description of a proposal in solid material and a template to be copied. A physical model stands between representation and reality, being both a representation of something and a tangible object in itself. Because of this, models have immediacy and can capture aspects of proposition that a drawing never can, such as changing light and shadow patterns or the feel of two materials next to each other. Unlike linear perspective, which allows the eye only one viewpoint, the model enables the viewer to move around and view it from many angles.

Opposite page:
Models
Image showing some of the models created during the project. The models are fragments used for testing specific areas and for photographing the interior. Contrast the quality of the interior photographs to the model itself.

Interior models

Name:
Villa Ordos

Location:
Ordos, China

Date:
2008

Designer:
DRDH

Models can be made of anything. Most sketch models will be made of thin card and glue using a scalpel and metal rule while a presentation model might be made of wood or perspex in a well equipped workshop. Remember, a model is a representation of the proposal; it does not have to be constructed of the material proposed. Many very successful models use all sorts of surprising materials, found objects and things recycled from other pieces.

Interior models differ from architectural models in two ways. These relate to the scale they are normally constructed at (1:10 or 1:20) and how they are viewed. First and most importantly interior models resist the abstraction that occurs as one reduces scale. Architectural models edit detail as they reduce scale, focusing on essential qualities such as volume and light. The resulting empty space can render an interior proposition meaningless and the designer will need to consider what other elements need to modelled, such as furniture, materials, people or even an external view.

Secondly, unlike architectural models that focus on the exterior, interior models give the interior precedence, often reducing the exterior to a blank box and only articulating openings such as windows and doors. This poses a question of how they are viewed as the viewer is 'outside' the model. Removal of a wall or ceiling is the most common device to solve this, but it is also possible to build walk-in models. The images shown here depict a collection of models made during the design for a villa. The main model was designed to be photographed to generate interior views rather than to be a model *per se* and it is interesting to compare the photographs of the interior to the model itself.

Drawing space

'There is in this country an orthodoxy that says every interior must be flooded with light. But actually an interior should be about a range of brighter areas near the window, darker places away from the window and towards the corners.'

Adam Caruso

Far left and centre:
Foamboard and card model
A luxurious villa for an art collector is designed to be experienced enfilade, each room offering oblique views to spaces beyond. A hierarchy of rooms created by scale and a material layering of surface.

Left:
Light effect
Image showing light at the top of the main stair. The brick effect is achieved with a photocopy.

Perspective > **Physical model** > Digital model

Concept model

Name:
Shadow House

Location:
N/A

Date:
2006

Designer:
Edward Jefferis, Georgina Hodgetts (second-year interior architecture students at Oxford Brookes University, England)

These are usually not to a scale as their message is qualitative rather than quantitative. They might be about light, texture, sound or an inspirational form. This model, called Shadow House, is constructed of laser-cut MDF elements of a house mounted on the turntable of an old gramophone player. As the record turns, different spaces come in and out of focus. The model is concerned with the experience of movement through space rather than pertaining to actual form.

Above:
Model
This model was constructed using laser-cut MDF elements and was mounted on the turntable of an old gramophone.

Right:
Rotating model
As the record turns, different spaces come into view.

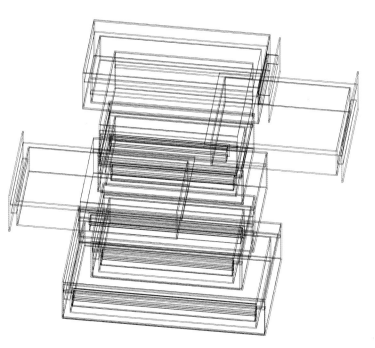

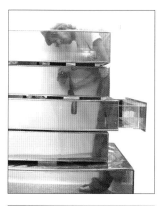

Prototype

Name:
Ghost Drawer

Location:
N/A (second year design project)

Date:
2006

Designer:
Naz Amraai, Laura Crew,
Ed Harty, Keiko Furukawa,
Emily Reitan and Marie Warren
(second- and third-year interior
architecture students at Oxford
Brookes University, England)

The word prototype literally
means an original type or form.
Prototypes are usually full-scale
mock-ups of pieces of furniture,
architectural elements or sample
surfaces used to experiment
with or test a design before
the proposal is built or put into
production. They are not the
finished objects, but test pieces
for a particular design issue.

The example shown here is a
prototype by a group of students
for a furniture assignment called
'Ghost'. They constructed a set
of box drawers from acrylic
and then covered it in reflective
film which, when exposed
to differing light conditions,
becomes transparent and reveals
the contents inside. Further
experiments included projecting
images on to the surfaces,
achieving multiple fragmented
images or points of focus.

The group drew working drawings
in order to cut the acrylic on
the laser cutter. However, the
reflective and transparent effect
of the piece would be impossible
to predict by drawing alone.
Photographs were then used
in portfolio sheets to record the
potential of the design.

Top:
Drawing
Working drawings were
created so that a prototype
could be cut from acrylic.

Above:
Reflective mode
When exposed to differing
light conditions the set
of drawers became either
transparent or reflective.

Above:
Transparent mode
The prototype in transparent
mode. Such effects could
not have been judged by
drawing alone.

Perspective > Physical model > Digital model

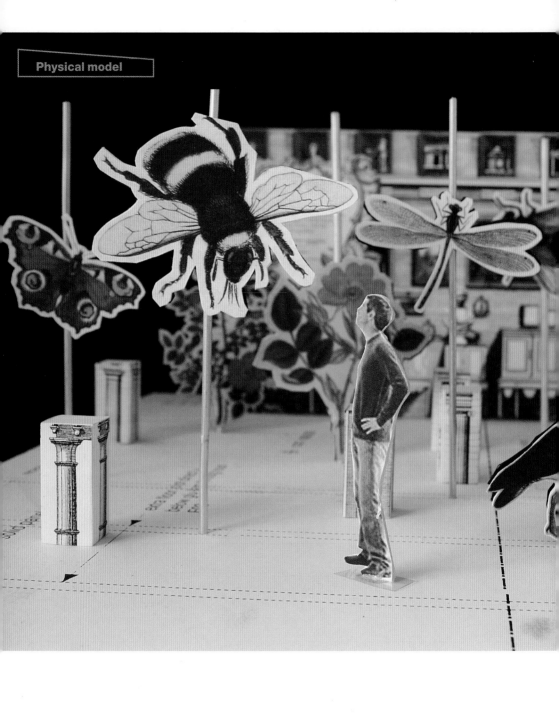

'I would not have the model too exactly finished, not too delicate and neat, but plain and simple – more to be admired for the contrivance of the inventor than the hand of the workman.'

Leon Battista Alberti

Tuscan

Sketch models

Name:
Flora & Fauna exhibit

Location:
Hardwick Park, England

Date:
2007

Designer:
Metaphor

Sketch models are fast to make, easy to modify and, if photographed, are a quick way of generating images. The one shown here is a sketch model of an exhibition layout by Metaphor.

The modelled elements are pinned directly on to a photocopy of the plan, which in turn is stuck on foam board so that it can easily be moved around to test different arrangements. The architecture is reduced to line and text apart from a fragment of the building that will be covered in graphics relating to the exhibition. The eye is focused on the design of the exhibition. A photograph of a person has been cut out at 1:20 to give the piece scale.

Above:
Sketch model
Sketch models are an excellent way of generating images.

Right:
Model and plan
The modelled elements are pinned directly on to a photocopy of the plan.

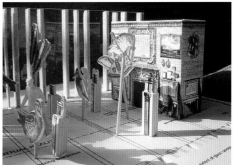

Perspective > **Physical model** > Digital model

Digital models are constructed on a computer using a computer-aided design (CAD) program or software specifically designed for the purpose. There are a wide variety of programs available and designers will increasingly use a range of software to create a model. Digital models were originally used as a visualisation tool at the end of the design process but today a designer is just as likely to use sketch modelling as a thinking tool at the beginning of the process.

Opposite page:
Sketch
These initial sketches were produced digitally, without any previous hand-drawn attempts.

Three-dimensional sketching

Name:
Dentist's surgery

Location:
N/A

Date:
2008

Designer:
Olga Reid (third-year interior design student at Glasgow School of Art, Scotland)

At the beginning of a project a designer will often use sketching as a form of visual thinking. It is an intuitive process that links sensing, feeling, thinking and doing, and everybody has their own techniques. Designers are now beginning to use the computer in a similar way to hand sketching, experimenting with trial and error rather than a CAD manual, although the results may look very different from hand-drawn sketches.

In this scheme for a dentist surgery Olga Reid starting by constructing the existing interior space as a three-dimensional model in an architectural CAD program Vectorworks. She then exported the model as an EPS into Adobe Illustrator, a program more traditionally used for two-dimensional graphics. Using the 'Blend' tool that allows one to blend one shape into another, she was able to modify the original model in a fluid, intuitive way selecting some planes, deleting others, sometimes multiplying more interesting shapes, playing with transparency or line thickness and sometimes just seeing what happens. The fly form shown is one of several results of this process.

Then, in a manner not dissimilar to developing a sketch in physical model, Reid rebuilt the model in Vectorworks, applying the surgery program to the form she had created and working out how it would be constructed. The final stage included returning to Illustrator to apply lighting, reflections, materials and people.

Drawing space

'Building, unbuilding, building again… very direct,
very 'physical'… We just build, construct in one-to-one
scale within the virtual space of the computer… no plan,
no section, no elevation… It's more like shaping clay.'

Thom Mayne

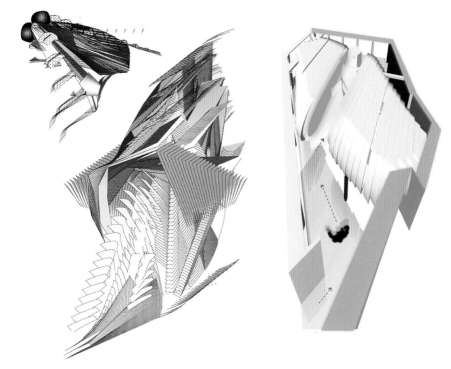

Computers

Until relatively recently, the computer was used as
a glorified drawing board to emulate existing representational
techniques such as plan, section or perspective. However,
as software develops and is more widely available, a digitally
literate generation has become more confident and the
computer is being used in increasingly innovative ways
to create design solutions that would not have previously
been possible by hand.

Physical model > **Digital model** > CADCAM

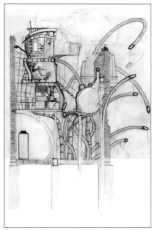

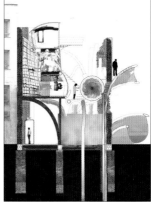

Above and right:
Original pencil sketch (right, top);
textured layers (right, middle);
hiddenline model in 3ds Max
(right, bottom) and the combined
layers as the final section (above).
The hiddenline model was made
prior to any of the other drawings.

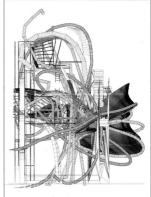

'Sometimes I see a finished building and say, "oh yeah, that was made using form Z". If you develop a project using AutoCAD which favours extrusions, it'll come out differently than if you used Maya, which replicates wave actions. If you're smart, you'll pick a program based on what's in your head.'

Charles Stallworth

Layering

Name:
Urban Villa, Brick Lane

Location:
London, England

Date:
2008

Designer:
Adam Holloway (third-year architecture student at Oxford Brookes University, England)

Traditionally, layering referred to the technique of placing one sheet of tracing paper over another in order to trace the design through. Today, layering refers to the practice of creating a drawing in layers in a software program with the ability to turn layers on or off. Many designers use a variety of programs and techniques to create their designs. The design process is often reversed, starting by using three-dimensional programs as design tools and then from these abstract models translating them into orthographic plans and section.

Adam Holloway developed his proposal for an Urban Villa in Brick Lane, London, by first creating a basic three-dimensional site model in 3ds Max and then applying the particle flow tool using the model as a constraint. The resulting computer generated services or 'pipe world' set the agenda for the proposal. The large section shown was created after the digital model and is a combination of the 3ds Max model, both wire frame and rendered, a pencil hand drawing and a texture layer added in Photoshop. The interior perspective is a photomontage created entirely in layers in Photoshop so could be described as two-dimensional.

Left:
Interior
Interior view created in Adobe Photoshop.

Physical model > **Digital model** > CADCAM

'Writing programs to create illustrations never makes much sense to students because they can be drawn much more easily by hand. However, as interactions are introduced, the difference between paper and computer become clear to students of any level.'

John Maeda

Parametric modelling

Name:
Great Court, British Museum

Location:
London, England

Date:
2000

Designer:
Foster + Partners with
Buro Happold

Parametric modelling is a method of defining a form as a set of related equations in such a way that when the values change, the parts change as well. Parametric modelling is transforming the design development process because it allows the designer to change the dimensions on one part of a model and to see the effects of these changes automatically updated in the rest of the model without needing to redraw or remodel the other parts. The speed of the process allows the designer to try many more solutions.

An example of the potential of parametric modelling is the redesign of the Great Court of the British Museum by the architects Foster + Partners working with the engineers Buro Happold. The proposal focused on creating a new internal public square in the museum with the restored Reading Room as a centrepiece. This was achieved primarily by the construction of a glazed roof designed to span the irregular gap between the circular drum of the Reading Room and the courtyard façades. The design teams were able to generate the toroidal lattice shell structure that spans in three directions by using parametric modelling. The final form is so complex that each of the 3312 triangular glass panes is different in size and shape and had to be cut by robotic manufacturing techniques. The project could not have been conceived with conventional modelling techniques.

Above:
The completed dome
The proposal focused on creating a new internal public space within the museum.

Below:
Structural lattice shell
The shell structure spans in three dimensions, using parametric modelling.

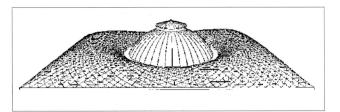

Right:
Lattice shell of toroidal and the dome roof plan
Drawing showing structural lattice shell of both the toroidal and the dome roof plan. The colour coding identifies the increasing size of the roof's structural elements.

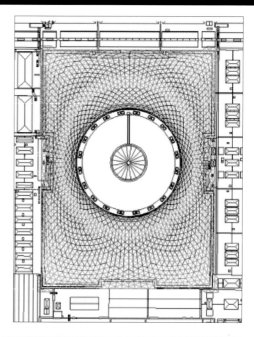

Drawing in code

Most software packages offer the designer user-friendly tools that are utilised by clicking the mouse. However, increasingly designers have started writing their own programs in code: a sequence of instructions made up of data and algorithms. The biggest difference in writing code is that it is a non-visual language so looks nothing like the finished object. Programming as a method of 'drawing' is becoming increasingly popular because of its ability to generate both multiples and surprising results known as generative form.

$$z/h = \left(1-x/b\right)\left(1+x/b\right)\left(1-y/c\right)\left(1+y/d\right)\Big/\left(1-ax/rb\right)\left(1+ax/rb\right)\left(1-ay/rc\right)\left(1+ay/rd\right)$$

$$\text{where} \quad r = \sqrt{x^2+y^2} \qquad (1)$$

$$z/H = \left(1-x/b\right)\left(1+x/b\right)\left(1-y/c\right)\left(1+y/d\right)\left(\sqrt{x^2+y^2}/a - 1\right) \qquad (2)$$

$$z/\lambda = \left(\sqrt{x^2+y^2}/a - 1\right)\Bigg/ \left[\begin{array}{l} \sqrt{(b-x)^2+(c-y)^2}/(b-x)(c-y) \; + \\[4pt] \sqrt{(b+x)^2+(c-y)^2}/(b+x)(c-y) \; + \\[4pt] \sqrt{(b-x)^2+(d+y)^2}/(b-x)(d+y) \; + \\[4pt] \sqrt{(b+x)^2+(d+y)^2}/(b+x)(d+y) \end{array} \right]$$

$$(3)$$

CAD (computer aided design) CAM (computer aided manufacturing) describes the process whereby a computer sends data to an electronic or robotic tool that then machines a specified material. It is a very precise method and the skill for the designer is in the design and construction of the drawing, not in the tooling. The systems discussed are expensive yet increasingly finding their way into practice both via students having access to laser cutters and three-dimensional printers at university and practitioners constructing the drawings and then sending them out-of-house for manufacturing.

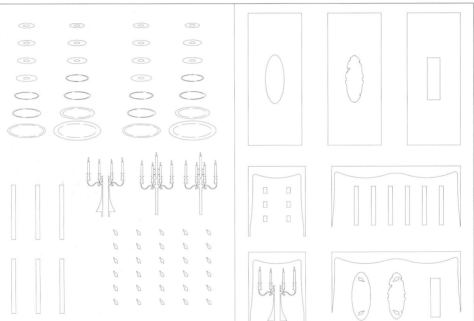

Left:
Assembled table
The Silhouette Dining Box was created as a 1:24 model of the designer's traditional dining set.

Top:
Laser cut sheets
The Silhouette Dining Box was created entirely out of MDF, ply and card.

Above:
AutoCAD drawings
These were sent to the laser cutter to be cut out.

Drawing space

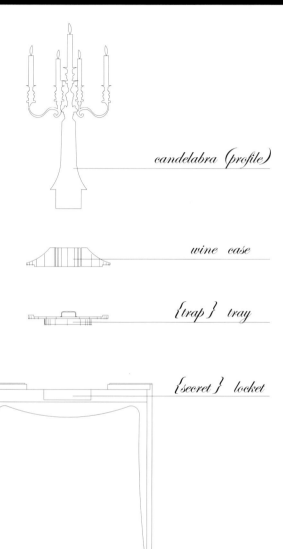

candelabra (profile)

wine case

{trap} tray

{secret} locket

Laser cutters

Name:
Doll's House project

Location:
N/A

Date:
2006

Designer:
Ana Araujo

The laser cutter uses orthographic drawings created on CAD to direct the output of a laser beam on a variety of sheet materials, which it can either cut or emboss. The precision of the laser allows for intricate incisions, complex embossed patterns and text that could not be attempted by hand. It is essentially a flat technique where drawings are laid out like a dressmaker's pattern yet when later assembled can model complex spatial arrangements. The skill with laser cutting is thinking in advance how the proposed model can be designed as a series of flat components and how they will then be assembled.

Inspired by dolls' houses, Ana Araujo created the Silhouette Dining Box as a 1:24 model of a traditional dining set as part of her PhD. Fabricated entirely on the laser cutter out of MDF, ply and card, the design celebrates the flattening intrinsic to the process, as it uses the idea of silhouette, shadow and reflection.

Above:
Assembly drawing
These show how the elements are fitted together.

Right:
The Silhouette Dining Box viewed through a peephole
The design uses silhouette, shadow and reflection.

Three-dimensional printing

Name:
Foyer and atrium

Location:
Moscow, Russia

Date:
2007

Designer:
Ron Arad Associates

Three-dimensional printing, also known as rapid prototyping, is another new technology that is finding its way into more innovative practices. Driven forward by the automobile and aerospace industries, the cost is coming down all the time. The process works in much the same way as two-dimensional inkjet printers. Instead of building up a text, this technology actually constructs a three-dimensional object by adding one slice on top of another in a vessel of liquid polymer (for stereo lithography) or powder (for selective laser sintering) that hardens when struck by a laser beam. Although limited by the size of the printer, it is now possible to translate three-dimensional drawings into three-dimensional models.

As a design process it is entirely three dimensional. The design is constructed in a three-dimensional modelling software package such as Maya. Once a form is decided on it is converted into STL files (which describe only the surface geometry) and sent for three-dimensional printing. The resulting model has an abstract sculptural quality that can then be combined with other elements to place it in context. This process works particularly well for more fluid organic forms that would be very hard to model with any precision by hand.

When Ron Arad Associates were asked to design the interior of a foyer area and atrium of a new office building in Moscow they used rapid prototyping as part of the process. The design was conceived as a 'carpet' that is pulled high up into the atrium space to provide a solution to the problem of the double-height space of the lobby and the vertical volume of the atrium. The carpet is a floor to walk on, a reception desk, a bar counter, a ceiling to the restaurant, a table and a piece of sculpture.

Above:
Rendered digital model
The same three-dimensional digital model can be rendered to give a sense of materials, light and the surrounding space.

Left:
Physical model
The main element, the 'carpet', was produced by three-dimensional printing and then combined with conventional model techniques to describe how it related to the space.

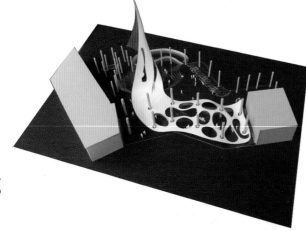

Above left:
Three-dimensional model
The carpet and office are shown
behind as wireframe.

Above:
Physical model
The carpet is tested for scale.

Animation refers to a temporal description of a project that utilises computer software to provide a virtual tour through a model. Using terms such as 'walk through' or 'flythrough', animation allows the designer or client to view a model of an interior as if they were inside it and moving through it. As the software improves it is increasingly being used as a design tool rather than for presentation visuals.

Three-dimensional visualisation

Name:
Design for a hotel in
a power station

Location:
Battersea, England

Date:
2004

Designer:
Ron Arad Associates

Three-dimensional visualisation is probably the area most closely associated with interiors. Using the computer to create hyper-real images that are more like photographs from magazines than drawings, these visualisations are created either in image-editing software such as Adobe Photoshop or by rendering (adding surface effects to wireframe models to incorporate colour, light, shade, transparency and texture) three-dimensional models. The sophistication of these images can blur the distinction between what is real and what is represented.

These stills are taken from an animation of a proposal for a hotel in the shell of the former Battersea Power Station. Rather than just show a 'walk through' of the finished proposal, Ron Arad Associates chose to animate the construction sequence as a method of explaining not just the spaces but also how the different elements fit together.

The model of the proposal was built in Autodesk Maya, an integrated three-dimensional modelling, animation, visual effect and rendering software. Maya is based on the parametric modelling described earlier and Ron Arad Associates were able to select and animate individual objects to show the construction sequence of the model.

The animation starts with the plan, then the service cores emerge and are gradually joined by the interior elements such as foyer and bar before the external envelope, coloured red, wraps them before your eyes. The tubular travellators clip on to the sides with the accommodation suites attached. Battersea Power Station appears as context before fading back again, finishing with a summary sequence which functions like an exploded axonometric.

Drawing space

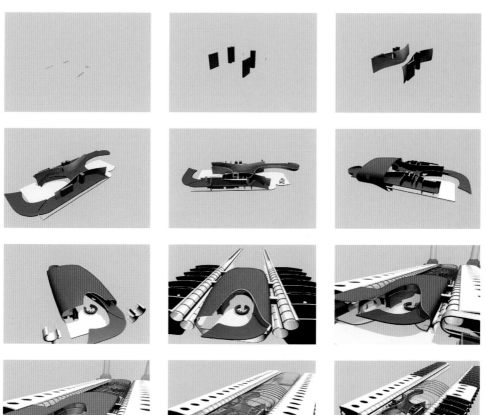

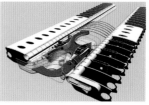

Above:
Animation stills
Stills taken from an animation
of a proposal for a hotel in
the shell of the former Battersea
Power Station.

CADCAM > Animation

Chronogram

Above:
Chronogram
The chronogram is produced using high-resolution photographs, elements of three-dimensional modelling and animation.

Name:
Space Time Drift

Location:
London/Hong Kong

Date:
2008

Designer:
Soki So (diploma student at Bartlett School of Architecture, London, England)

Animations require an audience to sit and watch and designers will often create a static image that sets the scene and gives a taste of what is to come. The word chronogram derives from the Greek words *chronos* – time – and *gramma* – letter – and is a graphic mapping of a film or animation. It should be understood on three levels:

1
It describes the timeline sequence.

2
It maps out the working methods of the film.

3
Finally, it should communicate the stylistic ambitions for the film.

Soki So lives and practises between London and Hong Kong, often operating in two time zones at once. In an animation, *Space Time Drift*, he melds his experience of the two cityscapes and interiors into one. The chronogram was created before the animation as a method of previsualising the animation, but it is also used as a technique to show the sequence of still images. Like the animation the chronogram is created using techniques of photogrammetry, combining high-resolution photographs, elements of three-dimensional modelling and animation to give a more convincing effect. The figure 'Hong Kong Girl' is added into the scene after being shot against a green screen.

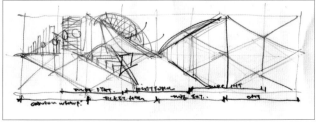

Above:
Storyboard from film
This allows the designer to prepare and experiment with their animation.

Left:
Early sketch
The designer's experiences of London and Hong Kong cityscapes and interiors are merged into one.

CADCAM > Animation

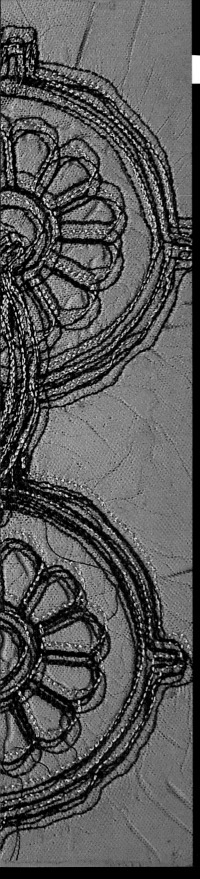

The effect, character or atmosphere of an interior is the most ephemeral challenge for the designer to draw. Unlike scale and proportion, which are both quantitative and measured, effect is qualitative and subjective. Effect can be fleeting, such as a particular light quality, or mobile, such as in the case of furniture and surface – rich in nuance but weak in character, its power should not be underestimated. The character of a space remains in the mind far longer than the more formal qualities, memory distorting the relationship between actual and perceived space.

Effect can be influenced by many different factors. In this section we look at light, colour, pattern, texture and illusion and give examples of how some architects and designers have chosen to represent them. There are no conventions in the same sense that there are for orthogonal or perspective projection and the examples shown differ greatly.

The drawings can be divided into two main categories: design drawings that experiment and test the effect and construction drawings that describe how the effect is built and experienced. The first category tends to contain spatial drawings often incorporating colour and material, and the second tends to focus on the detail.

Name:
Derry Playhouse

Location:
Derry, Northern Ireland

Date:
2008

Designer:
Tactility Factory

Drawing space > **Drawing effect** > Hybrid techniques

Light is one of the most difficult properties to pin down. It cannot be seen with the eyes, yet it allows us to see and can be felt. There is a paradox in the relationship between light and form. It is because of light that we can see form, surface and colour, yet it is the sculpting of form that makes light visible to us. Nowhere is this more true than the interior. Without an opening it is a black box; cut a window or use artificial lighting effects and it comes to life.

Below:
Mapping natural light
Series showing the sun passing through the interior. The orientation of the building, its global position and the date and time are all taken into account by the sun path feature. The model is drawn in SketchUp.

Right:
Artificial light – digital light
The same SketchUp model is used to show artificial lighting in the display cases.

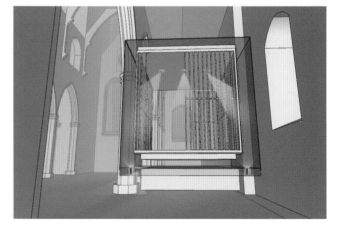

> 'When structure bends to admit light, that is when architecture begins.'
> **Louis Kahn**

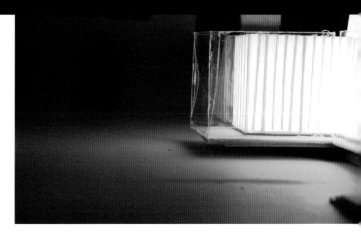

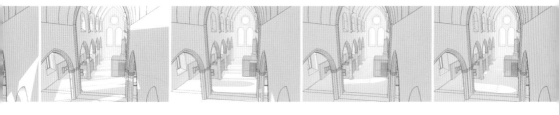

Simulating light

Name:
Museum of Garden History

Location:
London, England

Date:
2008

Designer:
Mami Sayo (second-year interior architecture student at Oxford Brookes University, England)

If light is invisible why does the designer need to draw it at all? How a space is lit both naturally and artificially is one of the major factors in how it will feel. Unlike the building that contains it, light is always changing and a room that is pleasantly sunny in winter can be stiflingly hot in summer. Likewise, atmospheric mood lighting can be unhelpful if someone wants to read a book. So the main reason to draw light is to simulate the effect.

There are two possible approaches: the first is to observe and record a light condition in an existing interior and try to recreate that in the design. If you look to the section on 'inspiration' you will find an example. The second possibility is to build the design in model and simulate the lighting either using a heliodome or, if the model is digital, using the digital sun path. As shown here, this allows the designer to view the way light falls within an interior over the course of a day or year relative to its orientation.

Top:
Artificial light – physical light
The physical model is used to show artificial lighting in the display cases.

Light > Colour

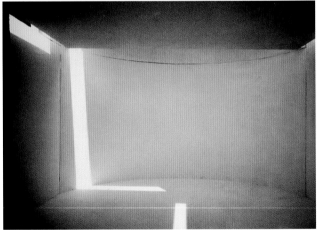

Above:
Watercolour sketch
Watercolour sketch by
Steven Holl.

Right:
Linear light
The behaviour of light in an
interior can be tested and
estimated through the use
of model and drawing.

Drawing effect

'Properties of light also provide the organising concept for the Museum of the City we designed for Cassino, Italy. We attempted to model the light on computers and quickly realised physical models were necessary. In fact light should be modelled full size as it falls off a wall at a square of its distance to the source. The galleries are organised in interlocking light sections. Between each section is an interval, which is the equivalent of silence in music and which forms a reversible sequence that can be played by bodily movement. Each exhibition area begins as neutral space individuated through its specific quality of light.'

Steven Holl

Sculpting light

Name:
Light score for Museum
of the City
Location:
Cassino, Italy
Date:
1995
Designer:
Steven Holl Architects

Many architects and designers not only want to simulate light to consider environmental concerns but also to test its more aesthetic qualities. Spiritually uplifting light has been used in this way since before the pyramids and the most memorable quality of many Renaissance and baroque churches is the use and quality of light within them. This way of designing could be described as sculpting light and requires experimentation with the size, shape and depth of window openings, but also reflecting and refracting light, letting it pick up colour and bounce around an interior. Making physical models and taking them outside and photographing them can be the most direct and simple way of testing these kinds of ideas.

In Steven Holl Architects' proposal for a Museum of the City in Cassino they made and tested lots of cardboard models. Giving each light formation a name such as 'curve-shaped light' or 'linear light' they went on to compose what they termed a 'light score'.

Right and below right:
Curved light
Holl's design technique could be described as sculpting light.

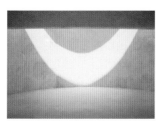

Light > Colour

Right:
Exterior of south wall
Note how windows appear as black openings.

Below:
Interior of south wall image
The same wall from the inside – the windows radiate light while the wall appears dark.

Drawing in shadow

Name:
Pilgrimage Chapel of Notre Dame at Ronchamp

Location:
France

Date:
1954

Designer:
Le Corbusier

In 1933 the Japanese novelist Junichiro Tanizaki wrote an essay on aesthetics called *In Praise of Shadows*. Widely read, the essay describes the difference between the shadowy world of traditional Japanese interiors and the dazzling light of the modern age, arguing that darkness is a difficult subject for architecture and design and its benefits are often unfairly stigmatised.

Shadow makes light visible and many architects and designers have used this to great effect in interiors where it is possible to control the amount of light and shadow. A beautiful example might be Le Corbusier's Pilgrimage Chapel at Ronchamp. Light passing through the coloured glass windowpanes pours colour on to the rough concrete wall openings. In drawings of the south wall from the exterior the windows are shown as dark holes in a white surface. In the drawing of the interior elevation of the south wall, the white surface of the openings is literally painted on to a dark outline elevation. The window openings themselves have been cut out of the paper and the location of the small coloured pieces of glass are marked with pencil on transparent tracing paper that is placed behind the window holes. It has been suggested 'as if the drawing could be held up to the light to test the effect of the design.'

Drawing effect

Below:
Drawing of interior
of south wall
The surfaces of the window
openings are painted white
and the openings themselves
are cut out.

'This was the genius of our ancestors, that by cutting
off the light from this empty space they imparted
to the world of shadows that formed there a quality
of mystery and depth superior to that of any wall
painting or ornament.'

Junichiro Tanizaki

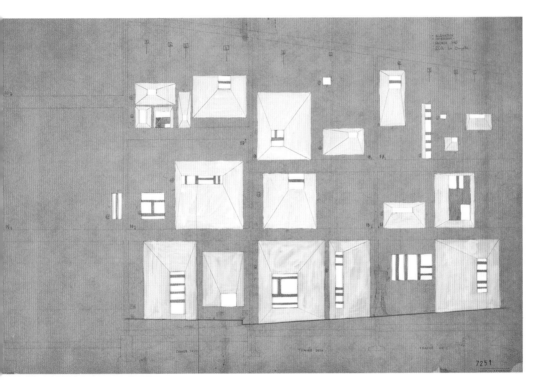

Far left and left:
Light detail
Pink and blue light is emitted
into the interior.

We see colour through the medium of light. Our experience of colour is determined by three factors: light, texture of colour surface (absorbent, reflective) and our individual ability to perceive colour. Each of these factors has many variants; a colour seen under a tungsten bulb will look very different to the same colour seen in sunlight. Sunlight itself is very different at different times of day. Generally speaking, early morning light is yellowish, becoming bluish at midday before tending to redden at dusk. So how can one start to draw something so ephemeral?

Drawing in colour: sequence

Name:
N House

Location:
London, England

Date:
1999

Designer:
Sauerbruch Hutton Architects

The architects Sauerbruch Hutton use colour in their work as a spatial medium rather than a decorative surface, believing one can alter a space entirely with a coat of paint. They have experimented with the ability of colour to create space through the juxtaposition of darker and lighter tones, or create depth with cooler hues against warmer hues. Quoting from Josef Albers' 'the actual facts and the factual facts', they explored the territory between space as it is visually perceived (actual) and the physical (factual) space of the building. In N House, shown here, the simple device of using large blocks of colour to form compositions independent of the original structure allowed the spatial limitations of the narrow Victorian house to be overcome.

As one moves through the space no colour is seen in isolation but rather in relation to the colour before and after it. The difference between the information given by the spatial sequence drawing, which shows the sequence of spaces and colours on the ground floor and beyond and the section, which describes volume and structure, should be evident. The spatial sequence is not to measure in the conventional sense.

Top:
View through to kitchen
Large blocks of colour allowed the spatial limitations of the Victorian house to be overcome.

Left:
View through the hallway
The architects used colour and the juxtaposition of lighter and darker tones to create space.

Drawing effect

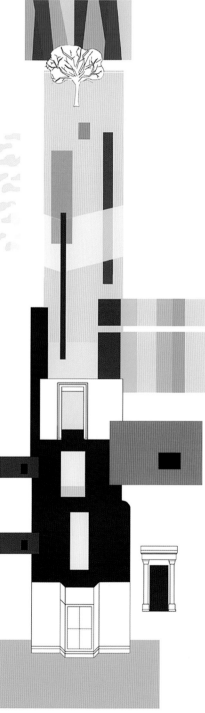

'The way Sauerbruch Hutton employ colour is not only far removed from any ornamental intent, it is outright anti-decorative – in their hands, colour acquires a presence no less defining than the physical dimensions of their spaces and the structural systems of their building.'

Kurt W Forster

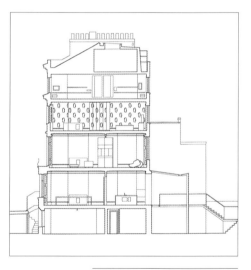

Above:
Section through house
The section shows the volume and structure of the building.

Left:
Ground floor spatial sequence
The sequence of spaces and colours is shown here.

Light > Colour > Pattern

Below:
Unfolding spatial sequence
to explore colour layout
In visual perception colour is rarely seen in isolation but rather in relation to other colours around it. It therefore makes sense to draw it in relation to these colours. Created in Vectorworks and Photoshop.

'Colour can extend walls, raise ceilings, and eliminate corners. Reaching beyond the limits of construction, it can sculpt a new space whose borders are defined purely by the spectrum, whose geometry consists not of carpenters' planes but of the lines where one hue begins and another one ends… colour creates an architecture all of its own.'

Mary C Miller

Right:
Plans
Basement, ground floor and first floor plans.

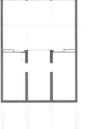

Far left and left:
Photograph of interior
The geometries of the interior
are articulated using hues of grey
and blue.

Drawing in colour: coding

Name:
Haus Marxen

Location:
Hamburg, Germany

Date:
2001

Designer:
Passe-Kaelber Architects

Traditionally having a supportive role in interiors, advances in colour psychology and a greater appreciation of its perceptual ability to transform space means many designers now use colour as a design tool. Form and colour are understood as two complementary but separate systems with colour used in discrete entities rather than splashed overall. Techniques include: 'symbolic' colour where a colour is used for its associative qualities such as Pompeian red; colour 'coding' where colour is used to communicate the different areas and uses of a space; and colour 'camouflage' where colour can be used to blend a new structure in with an existing one. None of these techniques come with graphic conventions attached. Designers are as likely to test sample patches on site, create concept boards with swatches or borrow from an image or painting as they are to draw. Testing and specifying the intended effect of a colour on a space can be far more challenging than drawing the form it should be applied to.

This family house outside Hamburg by Passe-Kaelber Architects was designed at the client's request as a 'house without doors'. The architects responded with a sequence of interlocking spaces incrementally increasing in scale. In order to differentiate between areas they used planes of colour relating both to use and atmosphere associated with those uses. Red – traditionally associated with heat – is used in the two kitchen areas while the cool souterraine is blue. The yellow shown in the photograph visually highlights the opening and bounces warm light on to the northern side of the building.

Colour affects our perception of spatial depth and Passe-Kaelber articulated the geometries of the interior using hues of grey and blue. The lack of doors results in deep spaces with no one room being read as a separate entity. The colours therefore had to be complementary. In order to test this the drawing shows all the painted surfaces of the house flattened on to one page and should be read like a developed surface. The painters later used this drawing as their reference.

Light > **Colour** > Pattern

The word 'pattern' refers to a coat of decoration applied to a surface, to a figure repeated indefinitely, or to a template intended to be reproduced. Pattern uses techniques of arrangement, fragmentation, reproduction and repetition and can be applied to paper and fabric as well as more physical materials. Pattern holds an ambiguous position in the mind of interior designers and architects and is loved and loathed in equal measure. The reason for this is that its effect is not just aesthetic but has an ability to convey cultural codes and challenge ideas of exclusiveness and originality.

Left and below:
Camo House
Created in Photoshop, Camo House is part of a series of images by FAT exploring the 'coding' of space under the title 'Taste not Space'.

> 'The evolution of culture marches with the elimination of ornament from useful objects.'
>
> **Adolf Loos**

Pattern as taste

Name:
Sint Lucas Art Academy
and Camo House

Location:
Boxtel, The Netherlands

Date:
2006

Designer:
FAT

The modernists rejected decoration and applied pattern as superfluous or even decadent. It was in direct contradiction to their call for 'truth to materials'. Much of the modernist unease stemmed from the belief that pattern was related to taste and therefore had the potential to go out of style.

Today pattern is back in fashion because of this ability to act as a carrier of cultural codes and has as much to do with the way we perceive our interiors as built walls. There is a blurring between the body, clothing, furniture and the interior. People are gaining an increasing confidence to choose their interior in the same way they would choose a dress or a hairstyle, and a new wallpaper might be one way of expressing this. In this fast-paced world architecture is slower to absorb change than the society that creates it and applied surfaces are better suited to reacting to style and taste.

Rather than rejecting this trend the architectural group FAT (Fashion Architecture Taste) argue that taste engages with important issues of class and value and therefore plays a far greater role in the construction of space than the spatial gymnastics favoured by the mainstream architectural avant-garde. Their Camo House project is an example of how our understanding of an ordinary house and its occupants is transformed by the application of a camouflage pattern.

Top and above:
Sint Lucas Art Academy
FAT were asked to create a new identity for the school and its existing 1960s buildings. The response included these patterned screens in moulded concrete wrapping the existing façade and colourful screens inside.

Colour > **Pattern** > Texture

Right:
Flight paths
Internal elevations and reflected ceiling plans of the mural 'Earth Major Minor in Yellow and Green', based on a pattern by Chris Ofili.

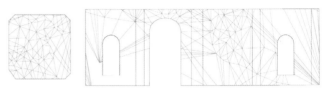

Pattern as effect

Name:
Nobel Peace Centre and Stephen Lawrence Centre

Location:
Oslo, Norway and London, England

Date:
2005 and 2007

Designer:
Adjaye Associates

Another force in the revival of interest in pattern has been new digital technologies, the scanner and large-scale printers. Patterns no longer have to be off the peg. It is now relatively simple to design a one-off pattern for a particular space and digital projection means patterns can be turned 'on' and 'off.'

Architectural representation uses two-dimensional images to create three-dimensional form. Pattern looks at the three-dimensional world and flattens it back into two dimensions. Described as a set of marks that have abstract powers, patterns are understood to underlie mathematics and our various conceptions of beauty. Many designers have looked to the more abstract qualities of pattern and applied them to buildings to great effect.

Artist Chris Ofili, working with architect David Adjaye on the Nobel Peace Centre, designed the mural 'Earth Major Minor in Yellow and Green' as a spatial version of the maps used by airlines to represent flight paths by drawing a line between different destinations. The triangulated pattern fragments the flat surfaces and visually separates the café from the reception area. In the more recent Stephen Lawrence Centre, Ofili again worked with Adjaye to create a pattern on the surface of the glazing of the west elevation. As the light falls through the windows it projects the pattern on to the interior: a dynamic mobile pattern.

Above:
Nobel Peace Centre
The pattern makes the flat surface fragment into shards of colour.

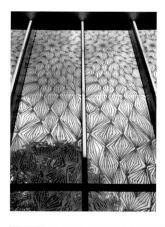

Left:
External glazing
The west elevation of the
Stephen Lawrence Centre.

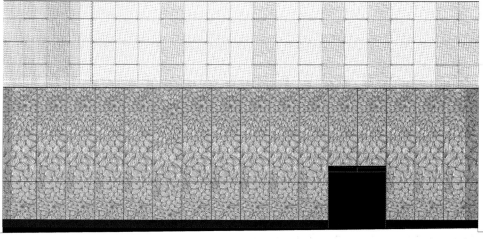

Above:
West elevation glass wall
Drawing showing detail of the
glass wall.

Right:
Pattern projection
The pattern is projected on to the
internal walls by the sunlight.

Colour > **Pattern** > Texture

Interior architecture is constructed out of materials, brick walls, stone floors, glass staircases – the possibilities are many. Depending on how they are detailed and finished, materials can be rough, warm, cool, smooth, each quality loaded with associations. Texture refers to how the surface of a material feels and is the most haptic and sensuous of the effects described in this section. Understood by its touch and smell as much as for its visual qualities, it has a powerful presence in an interior.

**Below and opposite page:
Textured drawings**
Alan Sylvester transferred photocopied concrete textures on to paper in order to communicate the textures within his design.

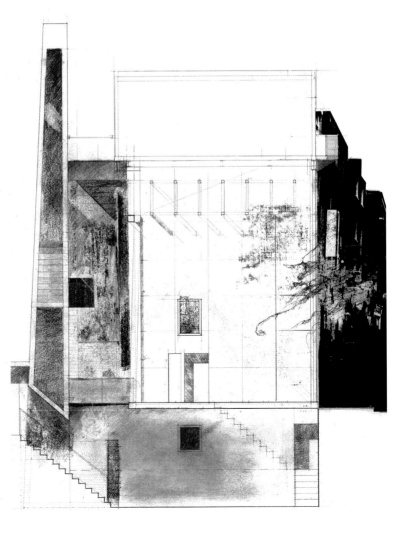

'I'm constantly developing my own philosophy, playing with textures and materials and contrasting modern, very technical features with natural elements. For example, glass installations/staircases placed next to sand-blasted oak, and pared-back walls enlivened with sheets of colour.'

Seth Stein

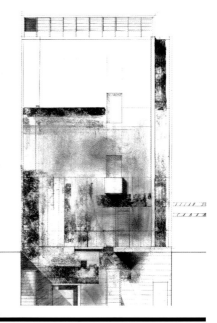

Drawing texture

Name:
Performance space and bar

Location:
London, England

Date:
1991

Designer:
Alan Sylvester (second-year interior design student at North London Polytechnic, England)

There are graphic conventions for most materials when drawn in section or plan. However, there are far fewer for describing the surface of a material if drawn in elevation or three dimensions. The most common technique is to collage materials on to drawings from material libraries found in the software. One must exert caution when applying these, however, as even if the materials are correct they often become overpowering at a reduced scale, making the drawing garish. Perhaps because texture is more sensory than visual, a level of abstraction such as sample photographs of proposed materials placed at the side of the sheet can represent the effect just as well. Text can be used to further describe finishes.

Other possibilities are creating your own material library from photographs of interesting surfaces, or rubbings made on site and applying them proportionally rather than overall. Remember that materials age over time. Architects like to talk about weathering on buildings, but for the interior the conversation will be more about wear and tear and traces of occupation worn on to surfaces.

As part of his design for a performance space and bar in Soho, London, Alan Sylvester proposed shuttered concrete to create texture and pattern on the internal elevations. To represent the texture, Sylvester used pencil on heavy cartridge paper, chalk, pastel, and transferred photocopied concrete textures on to the paper by rubbing acetone on the back of the copy.

Pattern > **Texture** > Illusion

'Sometimes things are planned, most often they just occur. We may focus on one thing but often it's "the other" that is more interesting – sometimes it takes a change of light or a repositioning of view to see the potential in a sample panel.'

Ruth Morrow

Drawing on the interior

Name:
Prototype panels

Location:
N/A

Date:
2008

Designer:
Tactility Factory

A designer cannot just draw a proposal; they must also have an idea about how the effect will be achieved. More experimental effects are best explored through the development of prototypes and samples with the best results being achieved through experiment followed by a more rigorous process of looking and analysis.

Tactility Factory is a research and development project run by Trish Belford and Ruth Morrow that aims to create innovative 'soft' interior products. It challenges the perception of textile and pattern as the 'dressing' to structure and instead integrates textile technologies into the production of building products such as concrete.

Through a process of making they are developing increasingly sophisticated techniques for combining pieces of fabric within poured concrete slabs. In the example shown, the linen fabric seen on the surface has had holes cut into it allowing the concrete to pour through to create the 'concrete petals'. In the 'embroidered concrete' example, the stitching on the surface known as the 'facecloth' is part of a multilayered fabric which is bonded back into the concrete by means of another layer buried below known as the 'substrate'. Other experiments have included using hybrid fabrics made of linen and stainless steel and also further working of the surface using the laser cutter.

Above:
Pouring the panels
Fabric and concrete is combined in the prototype panels.

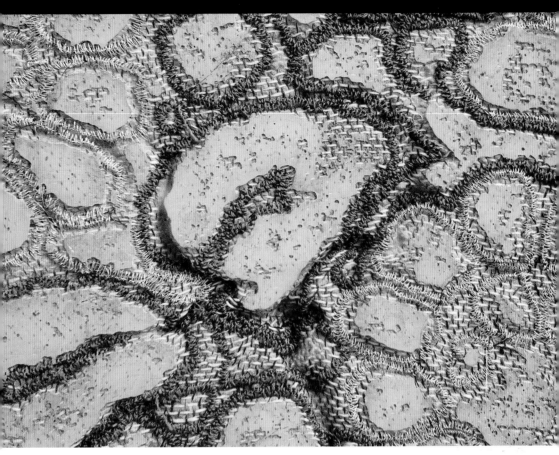

Above:
'Embroidered concrete'
prototype panel
Concrete with multi-layered
stitched fabric, using gold and
stainless steel thread.

Right:
'Concrete petals'
prototype panel
Linen, concrete and gold foil.

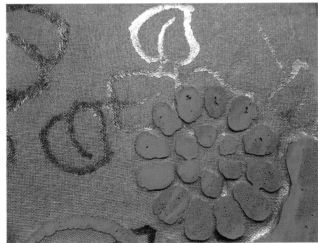

The perceived space of the interior, the 'effect', is predominantly surface and a proposal may be just paper thin, literally. In interiors it is acceptable to 'lie'. The modernist dictum of 'truth to materials' is pushed aside in a world of veneers, mirrors and concealed services. The use of illusion, particularly found in baroque and rococo interiors is very skillful, crossing the disciplines of architecture, set design and fine art.

Opposite page:
Fresco
Photograph of Andrea Pozzo's ceiling fresco of the allegory of the Apotheosis of San Ignacio, 1691–94. The painting, 17 metres in diameter, is devised to make an observer, standing on a spot marked by a marble disc set into the floor of the nave, look up through the church to Heaven itself.

Surface

Name:
Trompe l'œil fresco on the ceiling of San Ignacio

Location:
Rome, Italy

Date:
1690

Designer:
Andrea Pozzo

Illusion occurs when your eye fails to understand what it sees. It is dependent on your point of view; what you see from one position is not necessarily what you experience from another and the effect will to some extent be influenced by the social and cultural conditions in which it is used. Therefore as one gazes up at Andrea Pozzo's Vault of San Ignacio the viewer is not expected to believe the divinities portrayed in the painting, but at the same time has trouble deciding where the actual building ends and where the painted building begins.

The painting is a single-point perspective whose vanishing point is the Son of God and the ceiling is devised to be viewed from a particular point marked by a marble disc set into the floor of the nave. If one moves to another position the illusion begins to collapse and columns topple in an alarming way. Rather than seeing this as a fault, Pozzo regarded this as an 'excellency of the work'.

The enjoyment comes as you realise you have been tricked and marvel at the artistry, your spirit as well as your eye drawn towards the central focus.

In his two-volume treatise, *Perspective in Painting and Architecture,* Pozzo explains how he first drew the perspective on paper on to which he applied a squared grid. He then reconstructed this grid with string just below the ceiling of the nave. Finally he projected each square of the grid on to the ceiling by means of strings stretched between the viewing point through the grid on to the vaulted ceiling.

Drawing effect

'[I intend] with a resolution to draw all the lines thereof to that true point, the Glory of God!'

Andrea Pozzo

Types of painted illusion

Illusion: a deceptive appearance or mistaken perception.

Trompe l'œil: trick of the eye.

Quadratura: wall or ceiling painted to give the illusion of architectural depth.

Anamorphosis: a deformed figure appearing in proportion when rightly viewed.

Concept rendering ▪ Installation

01 Interior perspective

Drawing effect

Above:
Collage
Digital collage of site photos. This drawing was created in the early stages of the project as an initial intervention into the space of the derelict warehouse, using photographs taken on site.

Right:
Final proposal
The second image is a part of the designer's final proposal and looks at a more extensive transformation of the same warehouse, using ideas of illusion and playing with perceived and actual depth of space as one moves through it. Drawn in 3ds Max, leaving the existing warehouse as a wire frame and just rendering her invention.

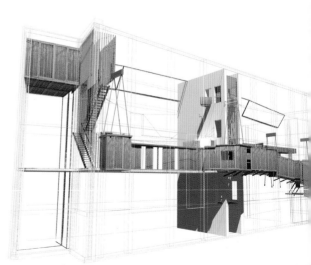

Struct

Form

Name:
Bargehouse Building

Location:
London, England

Date:
2005

Designer:
Wei Luo (masters interior design student at Brighton University, England)

Another example of illusion, this time constructed with form rather than surface, is the false perspective in Francesco Borromini's Galleria at the Palazzo Spada in Rome. Aided by a mathematician, Borromini played with the convention of one-point perspective using diminishing rows of columns and a rising floor to create a false illusion of depth. The galleria appears 37 metres long with a life-size sculpture at the garden beyond. In reality it is eight meters and the statue 60cm high.

Wei Luo combined the illusion of depth with the Chinese landscape structure known as 'lang' or covered walkway in her proposal for an installation in the former Bargehouse Building in Waterloo. Her installation provides a contemporary interior take of the traditional lang as it winds through the old warehouse, framing views but also distorting distance.

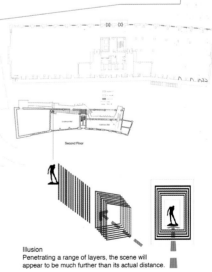

Illusion
Penetrating a range of layers, the scene will appear to be much further than its actual distance.

Texture > **Illusion** > Furniture

Interior architecture includes the design or selection of furniture and fittings: a (re)movable architecture that through the actions of user and time, reposition or change much faster than the more architectural elements. Furniture occupies a curious position in that it is both functional and cultural, the importance of which often usurps the need for comfort or convenience. This dual status is reflected in the need for two types of drawing: both measured drawings (often at large scale so it can be constructed) and more spatial drawings exploring its effect, location and arrangement in a space.

Built-in furniture

Name:
Denys Lasdun Retrospective

Location:
London, England

Date:
1995

Designer:
muf architecture/art

Built-in furniture plays a unifying role between the interior space and the objects within it.

When muf were asked to design the Denys Lasdun Retrospective they decided to frame the exhibition through the experience of making and using the buildings rather than just presenting drawings and models. The gallery space was focused on a 14-metre glass-topped table built in the shape of the plan of Hallfield School that Lasdun had built with Lindsay Drake in the 1950s.

Around the table and within it were drawings, models, ephemera, videos and interviews of inhabitants of his buildings. The table played the role of architectural model, an occupied building and exhibition furniture. In the plan shown opposite the many sections running alongside show the complexity needed to achieve this.

Above and right:
Final exhibition
The black and white photographs refer to the black and white photography used to record Lasdun's buildings at the time.

'A chair is a very difficult object.
A skyscraper is almost easier.
That is why Chippendale is famous.'

Mies van der Rohe

Below:
Plan of Royal Academy
galleries
Detail of plan of table
with cut marks indicating
numerous sections.

'Furniture is the servant of fantasy just as much as it is a response to practical everyday needs. The whole notion of the domestic interior as scenery for a play which we make up as we go along, and therefore of pieces of furniture as components in a constantly shifting and capriciously altered 3D collage, is propagated today in every interior decorating magazine.'

Edward Lucie-Smith

Loose furniture

Name:
Placebo Project

Location:
Various

Date:
2001

Designer:
Dunne and Raby

Today, loose furniture is usually off the peg and plays a dynamic or shifting role in the interior. Often chosen by the occupant rather than the designer, and rarely for purely functional reasons, its role can also be sentimental, a style statement or, in the case of exclusive designer furniture, its role is not unlike a piece of sculpture. Because of the complexity of the role if a designer is asked to develop a range of loose furniture the starting point will be prototype.

In their Placebo Project, Anthony Dunne and Fiona Raby developed eight prototype pieces of furniture in order to investigate people's attitudes and experiences of electronic objects in the home and in particular the electromagnetic fields they might or might not generate. The prototypes were developed as a family with a common language expressed by their purposely-diagrammatic form. Constructed from MDF and usually one other specialist material each piece referred to other furniture typologies and so are vaguely familiar.

In a process not unlike a medical experiment the pieces were then found a home and left with a trial owner for a month. At the end of the trial period the owners were photographed and interviewed about how the piece had fitted into their lives. The drawing, the prototype, the photograph and the interview could all be understood as descriptions of the project.

Above:
Electro-Draught Excluder
At the end of the project, trial owners were photographed and interviewed about how the piece had fitted into their lives.

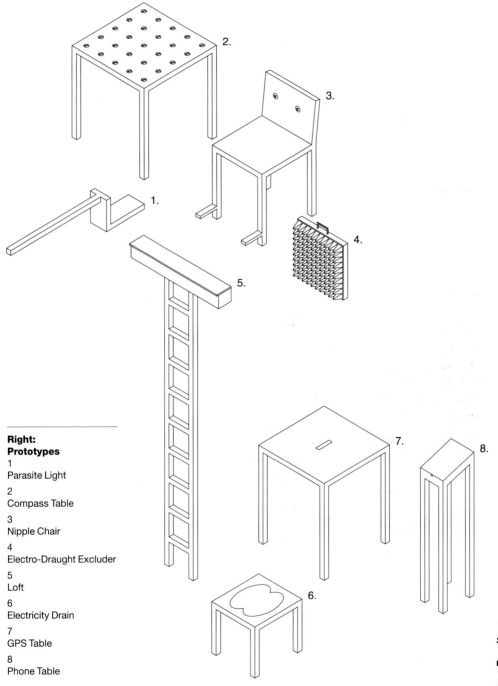

2.

3.

1.

4.

5.

Right:
Prototypes

1
Parasite Light

2
Compass Table

3
Nipple Chair

4
Electro-Draught Excluder

5
Loft

6
Electricity Drain

7
GPS Table

8
Phone Table

7.

8.

6.

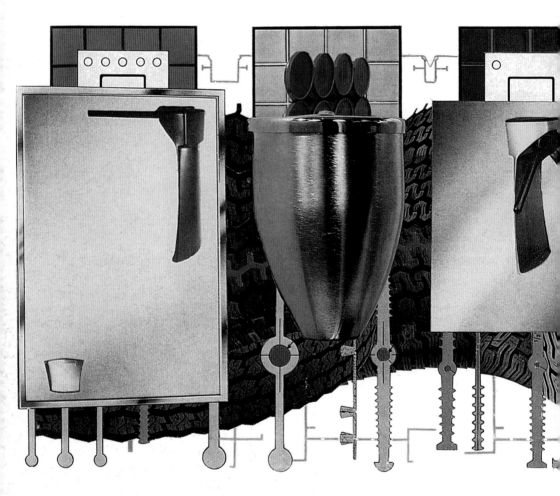

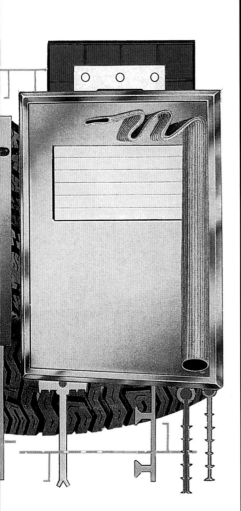

The final section looks at methods of creating drawings – which I have named 'hybrids' – that might use techniques from several methods discussed previously, or even techniques appropriated from other disciplines. Such techniques are not new. Designers have been using collage and montage borrowed from art practice or storyboards borrowed from film-making for a long time. Today, however, the scanner, the digital camera and software which is happy importing a variety of media have made the hybrid the medium of the moment.

Name:
Initial collage, Appliance House

Location:
N/A

Date:
1989

Designer:
Ben Nicholson

The term 'borrowed medium' refers to materials and techniques borrowed from other disciplines or practices. This section will look at a variety of techniques that specifically use either a combination of drawing techniques or refer to a practice not traditionally associated with the practice of interior architecture. What is interesting with hybrid drawings is that the fusing of the different techniques creates new methods of drawing. When this happens it is not only the graphics that fuse but also the ideas associated with them, so a sectional perspective is able to describe form and effect, a collage design will embody ideas and storyboarding as a design technique will be associated with movement and sequence.

Below:
Sectional perspective,
Daisy Klyhn
This sectional perspective was drawn in Vectorworks. Othographic section, digital model and techniques borrowed from other disciplines are used to give a sense of perspective, enabling the designer to show both form and effect.

Sources of technique

There are many sources of technique. Throughout the previous sections there has been a variety of hybrid drawings shown, the most common being the combination of hand and computer drawing. Other examples could be combining orthographic section and perspective in the 'sectional perspective' or combining line drawing and photograph. The photographs could be either taken of the existing site or from a model. Below is a list of the most common sources, but others might be archaeology, choreography, illustration, installation art or set design. Feel free to add your own.

From architecture
The biggest debt is to architecture. Not only the definition of what a drawing is for, but also the methods of drawing to measure and drawing space.

From art
Originally art disciplines provided perspective, illusion and techniques of describing three-dimensional space in two dimensions on a sheet of paper. Increasingly today, interior architects are looking to art practice for atmospheric effect drawings.

'I think eventually what we are looking at is a fusion. That is what we are trying to do in this office: fuse visual production with analog production, with thinking, with program, and ultimately what comes out at the end is not so clearly one thing or another; that's what we're striving for.'

Hani Rashid

From graphic design
Both for layout and what is often termed as information design, which uses words, diagrams, type and sequencing to communicate complex information simply and clearly.

From film
The film industry has given techniques of montage and the sequence/time-based drawings such as storyboard, as well as the use of photographing models like stage sets. Today animation created from three-dimensional digital models is blurring the boundary between actual proposition, film special effects and the game industry.

From advertising
Drawings have cultural references and codes which allow them to be designed and understood as a visual language in the same way as we read advertisements. Drawings give off much more complicated messages than just formal proposition and techniques such as concept board refer to this.

Borrowed mediums > Collage and montage

Set design

Above:
Entrance hall
David Connor's design is inspired by the cultural scene in London in the late 1970s.

Opposite page:
Design for entrance hall
Design for the entrance hall of a London flat for Marco Pirroni. Pencil, gouache and acrylic 1 x 0.8m.

Name:
Entrance hall for a flat for Marco Pirroni

Location:
London, England

Date:
1985

Designer:
David Connor

Set design is the practice of making sets and backdrops for theatre, film and television. Focusing on the more scenographic qualities of design, set design constructs a 'stage picture' to create atmosphere, give background information and generally set the scene. Interior architects refer to it for its ability to represent effect.

Designer David Connor's early drawings are of this tradition, directly inspired by the cultural scene in London in the late 1970s. The design for the entrance hall of a flat for musician Marco Pirroni is part of a larger body of early work based around a small group of influential London punks. The entrance hall creates a twisted, distorted space more like a drawing or a set than a domestic hall. Doors are angled and radiators tilted. A chair upholstered in real dog hair and a pile of dung on the floor complete the anarchic scene. As a contrast, the rest of the apartment is cool and functional.

Borrowed mediums > Collage and montage

Illustration

Name:
Land of Scattered Seeds

Location:
Graz, Austria

Date:
2002

Designer:
John Puttick

John Puttick's project *Land of Scattered Seeds* celebrates the poetry of small things and the ability of the individual to create their own space within the city, in this case by the use of nature. Driven by a fictional narrative, Puttick's design revolves around a series of characters on a street in Austria and their attempts to convert the exterior of their apartment buildings into a kind of urban farm.

Puttick's design is about growth, change and use. By using a narrative technique and by presenting his design in a book format, he is able to show how the design grows over time and how all the different users occupy it. The graphic references, both to the art nouveau drawings of Aubrey Beardsley and styles of illustration more usually found in fairy tale books, allow his audience to accept his unusual drawing style and enjoy the story, many not realising that they are being shown a design proposition in all its detail.

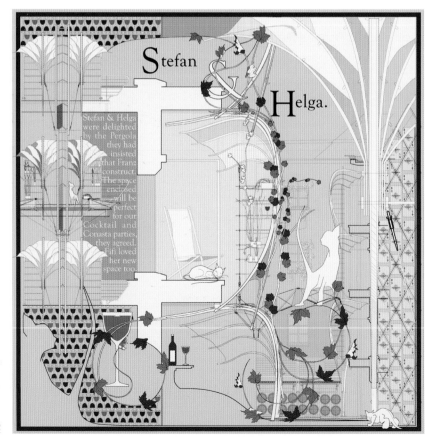

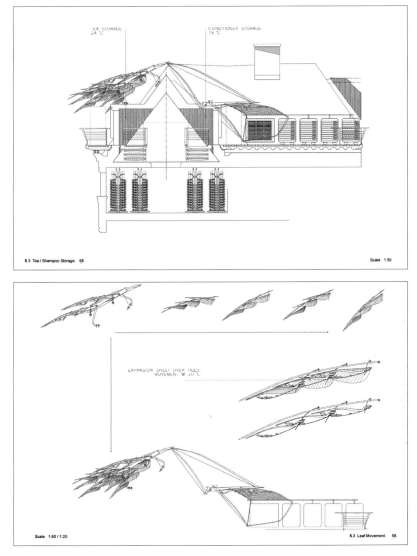

5.3 Tea / Shampoo Storage. 58.

Scale 1:50

TEA STORAGE. 24 °C

CONDITIONER STORAGE. 18 °C

EXPANSION SHEET OVER TILES. MOVEMENT @ 20 °C

Scale 1:50 / 1:20

5.3 Leaf Movement. 59.

Opposite page:
Stefan and Helga's pergola
Puttick's designs show how
different users will occupy
the space, even Fifi the cat.
Drawn in Macromedia FreeHand
(a two-dimensional layout
program), with hand-drawn
elements scanned in and added.

Top and above:
Detail drawings
Puttick's designs are all
about growth and change and
by presenting them in a book
format, his audience can enjoy
the story, without realising that
they are being shown a detailed
design proposal.

Representation is traditionally about using one medium
such as paint to simulate something else. The application
of real fragments like newspaper clippings on to the
surface of paintings was introduced just before the
First World War by the cubists Pablo Picasso and
Georges Braque. Photomontage came into being around
the same time. The discovery was that the fragment,
while still recognisable as, say, a newspaper clipping,
would also be read as part of a new image.

'To choose the placement of pieces, to relate parts, constitutes an architectural act.'

Josep Quetglas

Collage

Name:
Just What is it that Makes Today's Home so Different, so Appealing?

Location:
N/A

Date:
1956

Designer:
Richard Hamilton

Opposite page:
Richard Hamilton's *Just What is it that Makes Today's Home so Different, so Appealing?* was produced for the This is Tomorrow exhibition by the ICA Independent Group in London, England.

There is some confusion between the terms collage and montage, but for the purpose of the interior drawing, collage is a fine art technique that works at the level of the drawing itself, so might be used to describe texture or form, while montage is a filmic technique that is affected by the context in which it operates and refers to the wider culture beyond the drawing. They are both concerned more with surface and image than with space and form.

In his collage, *Just What is it that Makes Today's Home so Different, so Appealing?* pop artist Richard Hamilton uses collaged elements to make a comment on the idealised interior of modern consumer culture.

Starting with an image of an 'ideal interior' from an advertisement for flooring from the *Ladies Home Journal*, he proceeded to collage on to it an inventory of indispensible objects for the modern home. The ceiling is replaced by an early satellite view of earth, the fireplace with the television, and the black and white rug is an enlarged detail from a postcard of the beach at Whitley Bay in England. 'Adam and Eve', as Hamilton called the figures, were also cut from magazines – the body builder holding a lollipop was a well known model of the time.

Although the perspective of the original image remains intact, Hamilton chose the objects for their ability to carry a message rather than just creating a scene.

Ways of making, ways of thinking

Collage and montage can be understood both as ways of making and ways of thinking. Their construction is based on the selection, placing and fixing of fragments. The word collage comes from the French *coller* – to glue – and traditionally this is achieved with a scalpel and glue or editing tape. However, image-editing software such as Adobe Photoshop means the whole process is becoming digitised to the extent that the term 'photoshopping' is used as a verb.

The skill of the technique lies in the selection of the elements. This is an intellectual activity requiring the placement of one fragment next to another in such a way that the net result is far greater than the sum of the parts. This ability to see the potential of the fragment in relation to the whole becomes a way of thinking.

Borrowed mediums > **Collage and montage** > Storyboard

Right:
Collage section and elevation
These collages were created
from pieces cut from Sears and
Sweets catalogues. In taking
these fragments of disposable
consumer society and
transforming through such
processes, a proposition for
a bathroom cabinet is reached.

Collage

Name:
Telamon Cupboard,
Appliance House

Location:
N/A

Date:
1989

Designer:
Ben Nicholson

Ben Nicholson describes
the Appliance House he created
in 1989 as a 'sub-urban home
turned into a shelter from every
kind of consumptive adversity the
city is able to muster.' Nicholson
creates the collages from
everyday minutiae cut from mail-
order catalogues. The fragments
of a disposable consumer society
are then transformed through
a process of collage, photocopy
and drawing into proposition.
This technique of layering
images so a mirrored bathroom
cabinet becomes a giant wooden
Telamon Cupboard, a plastic
dinosaur becomes part of the
pulley system has been described
as almost archaeological in
its thinking, creating an interior
out of the objects or fragments
that the same interior might more
usually contain.

The Telamon Cupboard began
its life as a paper collage 'in the
guise of a mirrored bathroom
cabinet with an entrance turnstile
adhered to its front and numerous
other appendages dangling
from its sides. The cabinet was
nurtured through drawing to
reinvent itself into a giant wooden
cabinet of immense roundness,
stability and gravitational force.'

'The activity of collage, like every visual activity, can profoundly alter the way things and places are viewed.'

Ben Nicholson

Right:
Pencil drawing
By creating an interior from the objects or fragments that the same interior might more usually contain, Nicholson's method is considered by many to be archaeological in its thinking.

Below right:
Maquette
Full-scale construction of the Telamon Cupboard.

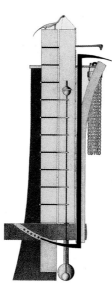

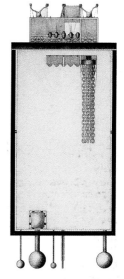

> 'Construction with intervals suggests that in montage it is not the elements that are significant, but the space in-between that defines the potential depth.'
>
> **Stan Allen**

Montage

Name:
The Institute for Illegal Architects

Location:
London, England

Date:
1998

Designer:
Jonathan Hill

Montage is a filmic technique widely used in both fine art and advertising, using images as allegory or symbols to suggest concepts in the viewer's mind. Simply put, A+B = C, not AB. Thus the image of a child and a mouth gives the idea of a scream, and the image of a bird and a mouth gives the idea of a song. Traditionally, photomontage juxtaposed shocking images for political effect but today the technique is so widely used in television, film and advertising, it is almost invisible.

The spatial application of montage is less well explored, the main difference being that montage cannot be controlled in the way it can with a two-dimensional image because the gaps between elements become as important as the elements themselves. These gaps are what give the image depth yet will shift as the occupant moves through space, the montage endlessly made and remade by each user. The architect and writer Jonathan Hill believes montage reveals one of the most important qualities of space: that it is made and not found.

In his allegorical project 'The Institute for Illegal Architects', Hill employs montage as a technique both to construct drawings and meaning. It proposes an Institute of Illegal Architects to be sited in front of the Royal Institute of British Architects, each institution questioning the validity of the other. Hill likens the relationship between the two to that between the body and the fairground mirror that fattens, thins and distorts the original – inviting both laughter and nightmares.

Above left:
Visual index of transient elements
Transient elements are mobile objects such as the table or even the architect himself, which move around the institute and each other in a constant state of flux. The juxtaposition is determined by the user not the designer.

Opposite page top:
Interior perspective
A glass sliding wall leads to the toilets, shared by RIBA and IIA. In the foreground is the table from the visual index of transient elements.

Opposite page bottom:
Exterior perspective
Exterior perspective looking north. One of the transient elements from the visual index is shown in the foreground.

Hybrid techniques

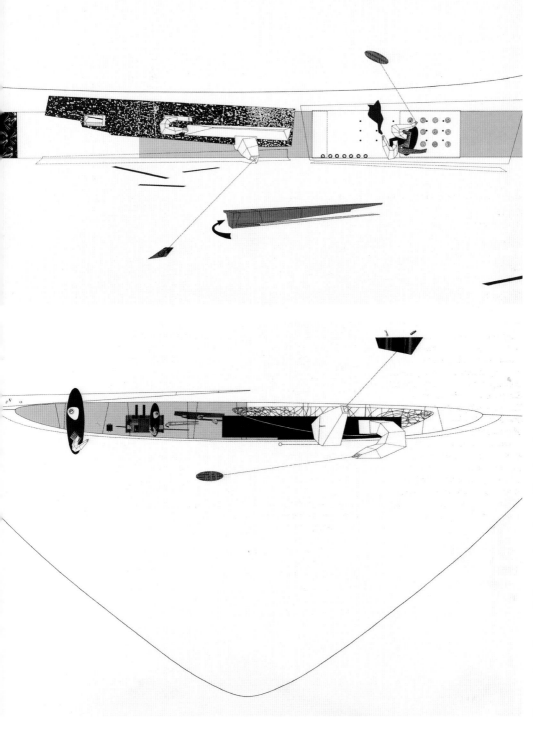

Storyboard is a technique borrowed from the film industry whereby sketches of camera shots are drawn out in sequence rather like a comic book. Functioning like a design drawing, they help directors 'previsualise' and communicate to other members of the cast before the scene is shot. Storyboards are a method of describing event and location in a time-based sequence. It is both a method of doing and a way of seeing and as such can be a useful technique both for designing and describing interior architecture.

As design technique

Name:
Spatial narratives

Location:
N/A

Date:
2007

Designer:
Dan Cox (third-year interior design student at RMIT, Melbourne, Australia)

Storyboard as a design tool allows the designer to work with movement and view, capturing a sequence of 'moments' before fixing a whole design in plan. For a generation brought up on computer games this can be a very creative and fluid way of working. It opens up questions about framing, angle of view and glimpses beyond. It can introduce cinematic techniques such as the use of 'familiar image' where, for instance, the good cowboy wears a white hat and the baddie wears a black hat so they can be easily identified. These techniques translate into a design language with ideas of coding spaces, as discussed in the section on colour, and are simple to represent. The example shown by Dan Cox uses storyboard as a method of creating a spatial narrative based on a film.

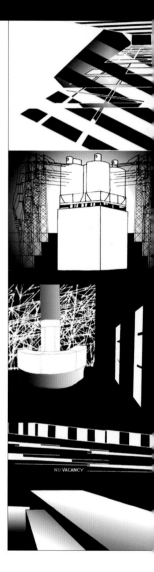

Above:
Drawing as spatial narrative
This storyboard was created
using preliminary sketches from
the film *Minority Report*. The
sketches were then developed
through model. The models were
photographed and these images
manipulated in Photoshop.

Collage and montage > **Storyboard** > Layout

Internal Views and environment

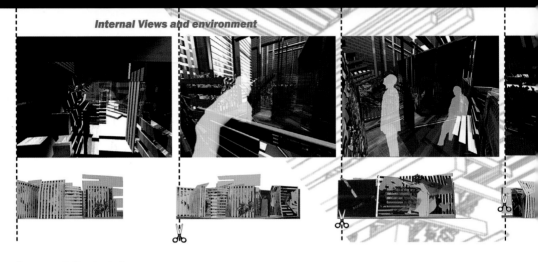

As presentation technique

Name:
Folding Pavilion

Location:
N/A

Date:
2007

Designer:
Harrison Gates (third-year interior architecture student at Oxford Brookes University, England)

Storyboard can also be used as a method of presenting a scheme as a three-dimensional sequence. This is particularly useful in designs where there is a narrative or predetermined route such as exhibition design. The storyboard can be laid out as a linear series on a sheet, as individual images in a document viewed by turning the page or even as a flip book. In the two strips for an exhibition design by Harrison Gates the advantages of the storyboard in describing the spatial experience in comparison to the plan cut-aways shown in the strip below are clear.

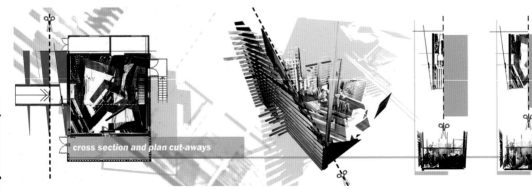

cross section and plan cut-aways

Above:
Storyboard
Folding Pavilion. The storyboard explaining spatial sequence of visitor route for exhibition of interior architecture. Views are selected using the walk through tool and individually rendered. The model was created in 3ds Max. Views were then opened in Adobe Photoshop and further manipulated.

Below:
Cut-away
Series of 'plan cut-aways' through model.

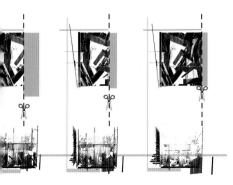

Cinematic techniques that could have spatial application

Separation: fragmentation of a scene into single images in alternation: A, B, A, B, etc.

Slow disclosure: the gradual introduction of pictorial information within a single shot, or several.

Familiar image: a stabilising anchor image periodically reintroduced without variations.

Multi-angularity: a series of views of contrasting angles and compositions.

Orchestration: the arrangement of the various other elements of structure throughout the film or space.

As must be apparent by now, no individual drawing tells the whole story of something as complicated as a three-dimensional design. So it is common to use presentation techniques that 'lay out' a variety of drawings, photographs and text. Layout can be on an individual sheet or a collection of sheets bound together to form a document or portfolio. Whichever it is, the layout of the elements is as important as the quality of the individual drawings and should be seen as a design exercise in itself. Layout demands many of the same issues of communication, composition, and cultural association as the design process itself. Like any creative process there are different styles – look at examples and consider the different messages they are portraying. Layout can say as much about the person who creates it as the work it presents.

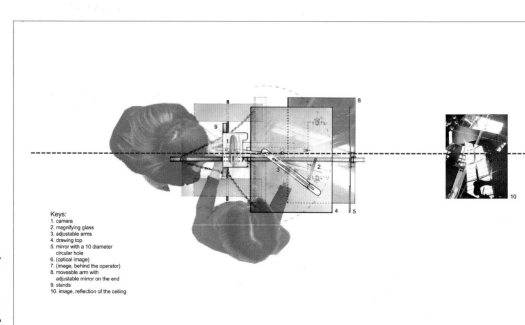

Keys:
1. camera
2. magnifying glass
3. adjustable arms
4. drawing top
5. mirror with a 10 diameter circular hole
6. (optical image)
7. (image, behind the operator)
8. moveable arm with adjustable mirror on the end
9. stands
10. image, reflection of the ceiling

Hybrid techniques

Single page layout

Name:
Viewing machine in Wapping
Hydraulic Power Station

Location:
London, England

Date:
2004

Designer:
Dan Deng (masters interior
design student at Brighton
University, England)

The first step is to decide what
you are trying to say. It may be
to simply describe the proposal,
but you may have other messages
to convey and associations
you would like to make, or you
may need to explain the context.
It is common to use a mix
of sketches, diagrams, plans,
sections, three-dimensional
images or photos of models.
Precedents and other examples
may help explain what you
were trying to achieve. Consider
what text will be needed.

You will most likely be working
to an ISO paper size (A1, A2,
A3, A4, etc.). The sheet can
be read landscape or portrait and
could have a colour or texture or
a background image. At this stage
it is useful to construct a mock
up page at 1:5 of the intended
layout. Decide which of the
images are the most important
and give them a dominant size
or position while reducing images
that are background information.
Think about the timeframe in
which the sheet will have effect;
this will probably be 45 seconds.
Therefore, use text for titles and
to highlight visual ideas, not for
lengthy explanations. As you
begin to place the various images
on the sheet think about the
composition and the relationship
of the pieces.

A grid of images will make the
pieces equivalent and be read
from left to right like a book;
a large or dynamic image
will attract immediate attention.
Images do not have to be
autonomous; try breaking
boundaries, overlaying images
and using text to connect images
and direct the eye. The aim is
to communicate your ideas as
powerfully and clearly as possible.

**Opposite page and below:
Layout sheets**
In these two sheets Dan Deng
explains an introductory project
to design a viewing machine.
She draws the machine in plan
and section, explaining the
device through photographs
of the machine in use, the site,
and explanatory text.

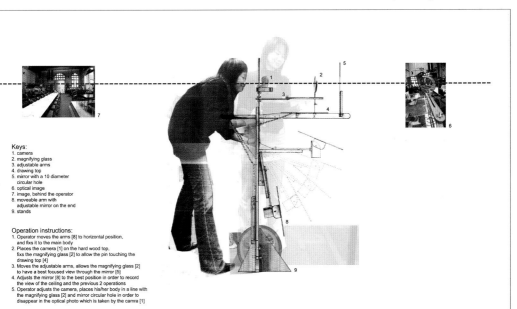

Keys:
1. camera
2. magnifying glass
3. adjustable arms
4. drawing top
5. mirror with a 10 diameter
   circular hole
6. optical image
7. image, behind the operator
8. moveable arm with
   adjustable mirror on the end
9. stands

Operation instructions:
1. Operator moves the arms [8] to horizontal position,
   and fixs it to the main body
2. Places the camera [1] on the hard wood top,
   fixs the magnifying glass [2] to allow the pin touching the
   drawing top [4]
3. Moves the adjustable arms, allows the magnifying glass [2]
   to have a best focused view through the mirror [5]
4. Adjusts the mirror [8] to the best position in order to record
   the view of the ceiling and the previous 2 operations
5. Operator adjusts the camera, places his/her body in a line with
   the magnifying glass [2] and mirror circular hole in order to
   disappear in the optical photo which is taken by the camra [1]

Storyboard > Layout

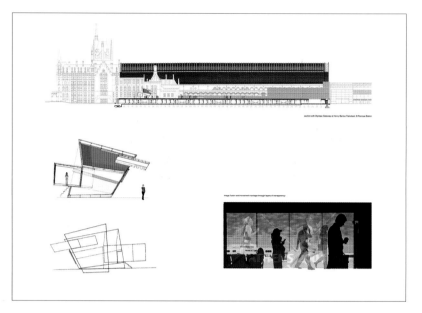

Portfolio

Name:
Olympic Gateway

Location:
London, England

Date:
2006

Designer:
Joanna Hunt (third-year interior architecture student at Oxford Brookes University, England)

A portfolio is a collection of your best sheets of design work arranged in such a way as to show your interests and talents as a designer. There is no single formula for the assembly of a good portfolio but it should be understood as a promotional activity and should be coherent and self-explanatory. Remember, different audiences are looking for different things. A portfolio for a college or university will need to show design processes as well as the final proposal while a portfolio for a client is more likely to show a variety of finished schemes.

A portfolio can be bound like a book, a collection of pages in a folder, on a disk or, increasingly today, a website. Whichever, it should be user-friendly.

If using a book or folder format, ensure pages are easy to turn and facing in the same direction as much as possible. If using a digital format, make sure it is easy to open files and to navigate. Your audience may not be as computer-literate as you.

Just like a book, a portfolio is read by turning pages, a double spread at a time. It should have a beginning, middle and an end and possibly a contents page and title sheets between sections. It does not have to be chronological but the sheets should be designed to be read as a sequence and should complement their facing page. Again, construct a mock-up of the pages to check the balance, considering what images are where.

**Opposite page,
right and below:
Portfolio pages**
By simple use of the colour
red the designer navigates
the viewer through plan and
section of a small intervention
in a huge space.

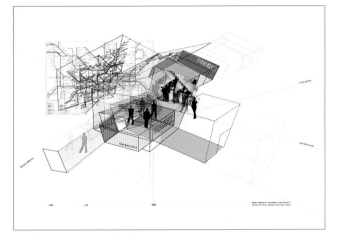

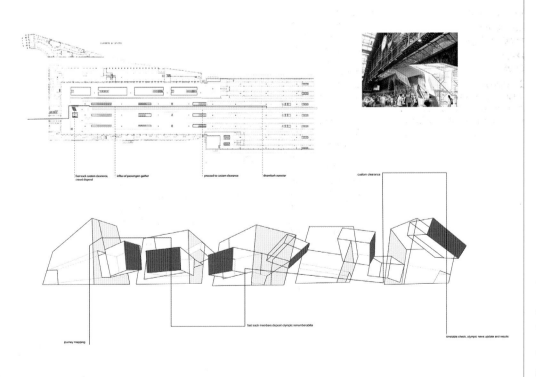

Final image

Name:
Multi-screen cinema

Location:
Rome, Italy

Date:
2006

Designer:
Sarah Khan (second-year
interior architecture student
at Oxford Brookes University,
England)

The last sheet in a portfolio
should attempt to sum up the
scheme. In this final image
of a proposal for a cinema in an
old industrial building in Rome,
second-year student Sarah Khan
sums up the project. Her proposal
was for a three-screen, three-
genre cinema, each screen with
its own entrance. The different
genres are indicated by colour,
form and image. In order to
show the interior architecture
the existing building and exterior
are indicated by wire frame.
The design sequence for each
genre goes from diagram to
form, leading the eye into the
final proposal.

Below:
Final proposal
The final sheet in a portfolio
should sum up the entire
design scheme.

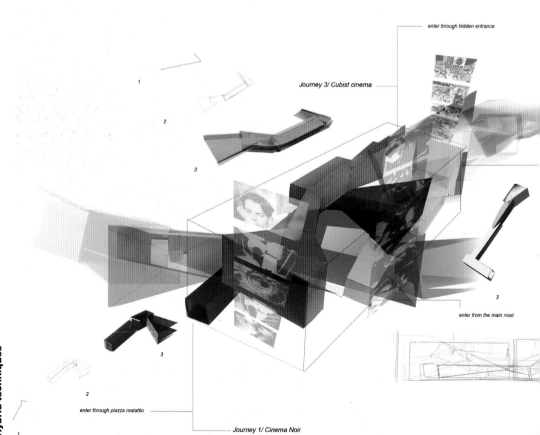

enter through hidden entrance

Journey 3/ Cubist cinema

enter from the main road

1

2

3

3

2

3

2

1

enter through piazza matattio

Journey 1/ Cinema Noir

Hybrid techniques

ele

Organisational tips

Document

Firstly, document your work as you create it. This will include storing sketches and drawings carefully, photographing models and installations and scanning images so you have a digital copy. It is important to choose an appropriate format (usually tiff or jpg) and resolution (dpi, or dots per inch). This means when you come to create a layout you will have all the material you need. Reducing or enlarging images, particularly sketches, can improve them, as can cropping.

Edit

Edit your work – you do not need to show everything. Layout is about selecting your best work and organising it in a way that makes sense. Less can say more. It is also good to show a range of skills. One drawing enlarged can be more effective than lots of small ones, and sketches or diagrams can explain the concept far more effectively than a complicated plan or section.

Grid

It can be helpful to develop a formatting grid or underlying structure to give yourself a template for positions and scale of images and text. With digital portfolios the layout programs will construct this automatically for you. Using the grid you can develop a visual element that is consistent throughout your sheets, such as a title or block of background colour to give order and connection.

Text

Think of text not as words but as a block that is part of the overall layout. Remember most pages will only be looked at for a few seconds so lengthy sections of text will not be read. Quotes can be a useful and elegant way to introduce a concept. Make a decision at the outset about font style, size and character: different styles have different associations and connotations. Try and stick to one, maybe two font types, and use a consistent size for titles, captions and body text. Finally, always check spellings.

y 2/ Cinema documentaries

1

wire frame elevation

Abstract A visual language or form that exists independently of visual references to the world. Usually non-figurative, referring instead to the concept or quality of a proposal such as redness, rather than looking like the proposition.

Analytical drawing A drawing that breaks a proposal into elements or principles.

Axonometric projection Placing a plan at 45 degrees to the paper edge and extruding or projecting the edge lines vertically to describe the walls constructs an axonometric, also known as 'paraline'.

Bird's-eye view As the name suggests, a drawing that views a proposal from above, usually removing the ceiling in order to view inside, commonly found in axonometric.

CAD (computer-aided design) CAD drawings are drawn on a computer using a program or software specifically designed for the purpose.

CADCAM (computer-aided manufacturing) CADCAM, or digital fabrication, describes the process where a computer sends data to an electronic or robotic tool that then machines a specified material.

Collage A fine-art technique that combines seemingly disparate elements to create a new image. Traditionally constructed with scalpel and glue, today image-editing software such as Adobe Photoshop means the whole process is becoming digitised.

Concept The initial idea or starting point that generates the design.

Concept board or moodboard The name originates from the tradition of interior designers fixing fabric and paint samples and possibly sketches on to a sheet of mount board. Today, however, concept boards are more likely to be put together in a layout program such as Photoshop.

Cut-away A drawing technique that 'cuts away' some of the exterior structure to reveal what happens in the interior. The cut can also function as a section and show the architectural construction.

Detail Detail drawing, as the name suggests, is the drawing of elements of a proposal at a detailed or large scale (1:1, 1:2, 1:5) in order to explore and explain how different materials fit together.

Developed surface or unfolded wall plan An orthographic technique for describing interior space where the five discontinuous planes of a room are folded out and placed on the singular plane of the drawing.

Diagram Diagrams are abstract drawings that use symbols or ideograms as a graphic shorthand rather than attempting pictorial likeness. Diagrams focus on specific attributes, editing out superfluous information for clarity.

Doodle A scribble or scrawl that is drawn while thinking of something else. Can on reflection be very insightful.

Elevation A measured drawing that documents the front face of an object. This can be an 'external elevation' or for interior spaces an 'internal elevation'. The edge of an internal elevation also outlines the section of the room.

Exploded drawing An assembly drawing that shows the elements of a design or design detail pulled apart. Exploded drawings are often drawn in three dimensions with lines, numbers or text to show how the elements will fit together.

Figurative drawing The realistic depiction of figures, objects, etc. (as opposed to abstract drawing).

Illustration A drawing or diagram that elucidates an idea or text.

Isometric projection Isometric works on the same principle as orthographic projection, but the plan is set at 30 degrees.

Layout Presentation technique that 'lays out' a variety of drawings, photographs and text. Layout can be on an individual sheet or a collection of sheets bound together to form a document or portfolio.

Maquette A small model of something to be made on a larger scale.

Material library A library of material textures in a software program that can be applied to a CAD model or drawing.

Model An architect's plan or design; a preliminary solid representation, generally small, or in plastic material, to be followed in construction; something to be copied; a pattern; an imitation of something on a smaller scale.

Montage Montage is a technique used in film editing that refers both to splicing sections of film together and combining images in a single shot. When used in the individual shot it is also known as photomontage.

Observational drawing A drawing that is based on observation of something that exists.

Orthographic projection Orthographic projection is a geometrical technique of projecting lines at right angles between a picture plane and an object, usually a building. The projection lines are parallel and the resulting image has no perspective.

Overlay Traditionally the technique of layering one sheet of tracing paper over another in order to trace the design through. Today layering can be drawn in a software program with the ability to turn layers on or off.

Perspective The easiest way to understand perspective is if one thinks of a piece of glass inserted between the designer and the object they wish to draw. The image is then traced on the glass.

Plan A horizontal measured cut through a structure, space, or object. In buildings, the plan is typically cut about a metre above the floor plane looking down (or for a ceiling plan looking up). However, a plan can be cut at any desired height for the purpose of design, representation or investigation.

Portfolio A folder or case for protecting, carrying and presenting drawings. Today, it can also easily be a CD, a website or a purpose-designed package.

Presentation models Models for presentation to a client, a gallery or possibly competition entry. They are often made by a professional model-maker, with a greater degree of 'realism' than the other types of model.

Presentational drawing Drawings for presentation to a client, a gallery or possibly competition entry. Greater care should be taken with layout, title, text and it should be understandable to the layperson.

Proportion The relationship of one thing to another in terms of size. Rather than defining elements by a measurement, it describes dimensions in relationship to other dimensions so they can be applied at any scale.

Propositional drawing A drawing that describes a design idea yet to be constructed.

Prototype Prototypes are usually full-scale mock-ups of pieces of furniture, architectural elements or sample surfaces used to experiment with or test the design before the proposal is built or put into production.

Render Traditionally referring to adding colour to a drawing. Today rendering is the process of adding surface effects to computer wire-frame models to incorporate colour, lighting, shade, transparency and texture.

Scale A graduated series or order.

Scale model A model of something made in a reduced size but to accurate proportions.

Section A vertical measured cut through a structure, space or object. The section is generally cut through the centre of the space but can be cut at any point along the plan.

Sectional perspective A technique combining the two-dimensional section and three-dimensional perspective describing, therefore, both form and effect.

Sketch A drawing – slight, rough, or without detail – especially as a study towards a final.

Specification Some documents such as specifications and schedules of parts, which form part of a drawing package.

Storyboard Storyboard is a technique borrowed from the film industry where sketches of camera shots are drawn out in sequence rather like a comic book and are a method of describing event and location in a time-based sequence.

Survey Survey or record of a building in its 'existing condition'.

Template A guide used to cut or trace a form; a model of a form from which others are produced.

Three-dimensional printing Or rapid prototyping. A three-dimensional object is constructed by adding one slice on top of another in a vessel of liquid polymer (for stereo lithography) or powder (for selective laser sintering), which hardens when struck by a laser beam.

Working drawing Also known as technical drawing, this is a detail or design drawing that is used in the design or construction process to illustrate the scheme to clients, regulatory bodies or publications.

Worm's-eye view A drawing from below, up through the floor, commonly found in axonometric drawings.

X-ray view A drawing where the viewer is able to look through a wall or ceiling, etc. with techniques such as dashed lines to show what lies behind.

Ro Spankie would like to give special thanks to her researcher Lynsey Brough, without whose help this book would not have been possible. Thanks also to the Reinvention Centre at Oxford Brookes University for granting her a URSS Scholarship to do this.

She would also like to thank Andrea Placidi, Alan Sylvester, Abi Abdolwahabi and Matt Clay and the Interiors team at Oxford Brookes University for discussions, insights and lively debate; Jonathan Hill and Lesley Lokko for advice and Philip Steadman and Helena Webster for reading sections of the text.

Thanks also to John McGill for his elegant design; to Suzie Attiwill, Graeme Brooker, Andy Milligan and all at AVA Publishing: Brian Morris, Caroline Walmsley and in particular, Leafy Robinson for her guidance and support.

Finally, Ro would like to thank Laurie and Noli for teaching her to draw all over again and Mark Lumley for talking of other things.

A book on representation must by its nature contain many drawings so thanks are owed to the many architectural practices and students and individuals who contributed images and drawings and ideas.

046+047: courtesy of Jonathon Connolly, Daniel Rosbottom and David Howarth
048: sketch (top) © FLC/ADAGP, Paris and DACS, London 2008, image supplied courtesy of Fondation Le Corbusier; diagram (bottom) by Mami Sayo
049: photograph by Matt Clay
050: sketches © FLC/ADAGP, Paris and DACS, London 2008, image supplied courtesy of Fondation Le Corbusier
051: photograph by Matt Clay
052+053: courtesy of Penelope Haralambidou
054+055: courtesy of Silvia Ullmayer, photographs by Killian O'Sullivan
057: photograph by Graeme Brooker; diagram by Aaron Losada
058+059: Kiasma Museum of Contemporary Art, Helsinki, Finland 1992–1998 © Steven Holl Architects
060: courtesy of Project Orange and Studio Myerscough
064+065: photographs by Studio AU, courtesy of Clare Cardinal-Pett
066: RIBA Library Drawings Collection
069: photographs courtesy of Max Dewdney
070: courtesy of Lauren Skogstad and Julieanna Preston
073: by courtesy of the Trustees of Sir John Soane's Museum
074+075: courtesy of Ammar Eloueini
078+079: courtesy of Sauerbruch Hutton Architects, photograph by Charles Stebbings
080+081: courtesy of Alvar Aalto Museum, Finland
082+083: courtesy of Prewett Bizley Architects

084+085: photograph by Leigh Simpson; diagrams courtesy of Architype
086–089: courtesy of Roger Kemp and McGlashan Everist
090+091: courtesy of Dr Victoria Watson
092+093: 'Art Impact, Collective Retinal Memory' © Maurice Benayoun, 2000
094+095: courtesy of Philip Steadman
096+097: © (30 April 2009) The Museum of Modern Art/Scala, Florence
098+099: courtesy of Dr Victoria Watson
101: courtesy of DRDH
102: photographs by Marco Casselli
103: courtesy of Ed Harty
104: courtesy of Metaphor
107: courtesy of Olga Reid and Drew Plunkett
108+109: courtesy of Adam Holloway and Toby Shew
110+111: painting by Ben Johnson, all rights reserved DACS; drawings courtesy of Foster + Partners
112+113: courtesy of Ana Araujo
114+115: courtesy of Ron Arad Associates
116+117: courtesy of Ron Arad Associates
118+119: courtesy of Soki So and Nic Clear
120+121: courtesy of Trish Belford and Ruth Morrow at Girli Concrete
122+123: courtesy of Mami Sayo
124+125: Museum of the City, Cassino, Italy, 1996 © Steven Holl Architects
126+127: drawing © FLC/ADAGP, Paris and DACS, London 2008, image supplied courtesy of Fondation Le Corbusier; photographs by Ro Spankie

128: photographs by Hélène Binet
129: courtesy of Sauerbruch Hutton Architects
130+131: photographs by Haus Marxen; drawing courtesy of Ulrike Passe
132+133: courtesy of FAT
134: photograph by Timothy Soar; drawing courtesy of Adjaye Associates
135: photograph by Lyndon Douglas; drawing courtesy of Adjaye Associates
136+137: courtesy of Alan Sylvester
138+139: courtesy of Trish Belford and Ruth Morrow at Girli Concrete
141: photograph by Alex Gore
142+143: courtesy of Wei Luo and Frank O'Sullivan
144+145: courtesy of muf architecture/art
146+147 courtesy of Dunne and Raby, photograph by Jason Evans
148: courtesy of Ben Nicholson
151: courtesy of Daisy Klyhn and Graeme Brooker
152+153: courtesy of David Connor
154+155: courtesy of John Puttick
156+157: © Richard Hamilton. All Rights Reserved, DACS 2008. Image supplied courtesy of Tate, London
158+159: courtesy of Ben Nicholson
160+161: courtesy of Jonathan Hill
162+163: courtesy of Dan Cox and Roger Kemp
164+165: courtesy of Harrison Gates and Andrea Placidi
166+167: courtesy of Dan Deng and Frank O'Sullivan
168+169: courtesy of Joanna Hunt
170: courtesy of Sarah Khan

Acknowledgements

Pull quotes

013: Loos, A. 1982. *Spoken into the Void: Collected Essays, 1897–1900*. Cambridge, MA: MIT Press

015: Owen Moss, E. 1999. *Gnostic Architect*. New York: The Monacelli Press

017: Evans, R. 1997. *Translations from Drawing to Building*. Cambridge, MA: MIT Press

018: Scarpa, C. *In*: Noever, P. (ed.) 2003. *The Craft of Architecture*. Vienna: Hatje Cantz Publishers

021: Aalto, A. 1978. *Sketches*. Cambridge, MA: MIT Press

023: Cook, P. 1987. Architecture and Drawing: Editing and Refinement. *Architects Journal*.

027: Fisher, T. *In*: Moon, K. 2005. *The Architect and the Model*. New York: The Monacelli Press

029: Rhowbotham, K. 1995. *Form to Programme*. London: Black Dog Publishing

030: Soane, J. 1809. Royal Academy Lecture 1

035: Koolhaas, R. 1995. *SMLXL*. Rotterdam: 010 Publishers

039: Berger, J. 1984. *And Our Faces, My Heart, Brief as Photos*. New York: Vintage

040: Pawley, M. 1968. *The Strange Death of Architectural Criticism*. London: Black Dog Publishing

045: Valery, P. *In*: Holl, S. 2000. *Parallax*. Basel: Birkhauser

047: Blake, W. *In*: Forseth, K. 1991. *Rendering the Visual Field Illusion Becomes Reality*. New York: Reinhold

049: Evans, R. 1995. *The Projective Cast: Architecture and its Three Geometries*. Cambridge, MA: MIT Press

051: Le Corbusier, E. J. *In*: Crowe, N. and Laseau, P. 1986. *Visual Notes for Architects and Designers*. Chichester: Wiley

057: Eisenman, P. 1999. *Diagram Diaries*. London: Thames & Hudson

063: *Sketches of Frank Gehry*. Animated film. Directed by Sydney POLLACK Culver City: Sony Pictures. 2006.

065: Zumthor, P. 2006. *Thinking Architecture*. Basel: Birkhauser

067: Gray, E. *In*: Frank, K. and Lepori, B. 2007. *Architecture from the inside out*. Chichester: Wiley

068: Rhowbatham, K. [source unavailable]

071: Loos, A. [source unavailable]

075: Koolhaas, R. 1995. *SMLXL*. Rotterdam: 010 Publishers

077: Allen, S. 2000. *Practice Architecture, Technique and Representation*. London: Routledge

079: Semper, G. *In*: Sauerbruch Hutton Architects. 2006. *On Colour and Space*. Baden: Lars Muller Publishers

081: Zumthor, P. 2006. *Thinking Architecture*. Basel: Birkhauser

083: Bizley, G. 2008. *Architecture in Detail*. Oxford: Architectural Press

084: Frascari, M. 1984. The tell-tale detail. *VIV*. 7. p36.

087: Brooker, G. and Stone, S. 2007. *Basics Interior Architecture: Form + Structure*. Lausanne: AVA Publishing

089: Kemp, R. 2006. *Negotiating Space – An Interior Practice*. RMIT University masters paper

101: Caruso, A.

105: Battista Alberti, L.

107: Mayne, T. *In*: Forty, A. 2000. *Words and Buildings*. London: Thames & Hudson

109: Stallworth, C.

110: Maeda, J.

123: Kahn, L. *In*: McCarter, R. 2005. *Louis Kahn*. London: Phaidon

125: Holl, S. 2000. *Parallax*. New York: Princeton Architectural Press

127: Tanizaki, J.

129: Forster, K. W. *In*: Sauerbruch Hutton Architects. 1999. WYSIWYG. London: AA Publications

130: Miller, M. C. 1997. *Color for Interior Architecture*. Chichester: Wiley

133: Loos, A. [source unavailable]

135: Balmond, C. [source unavailable]

137: Stein, S. [source unavailable]

138: Morrow, R. 1994. http://girliconcrete.blogspot.com

141: Pozza, A. [source unavailable]

145: van der Rohe, M. 1957. In an interview with *Time Magazine*. 18 Feb

146: Lucie-Smith, E. 1979. *Furniture: A Concise History*. London: Thames & Hudson

151: Rashid, H. *In*: Moon, K. 2000. *The Architect and the Model*. New York: The Montacelli Press

157: Quetglas, J. 2001. *Fear of Mies van der Rohe's Pavilion in Barcelona*. Basel: Birkhauser

159: Nicholson, B. 1990. *Appliance House*. Cambridge, MA: MIT Press

160: Allen, S. 2000. *Practice Architecture, Technique and Representation*. London: Routledge